"I GAVE UP in 1998 and had to be talked into doing one show. Two friends called and said you know you really should do this show. I said 'no, no, no, I keep losing my job, I been homeless.' I got a good job like my mama say, 'get you a good job making three or four hundred dollars a week and some benefits and you'll be great' that was her dream for me. So I said 'no, no, no,' and I argued and yelled and cursed and screamed at my friends and I did that one show in 1998 at The House of Blues March 12th . . . CHANGED MY LIFE . . . SOLD OUT."

—Tyler Perry
Visionaries: Inside the Creative Mind
OWN Network 2011

NEVER
Would Have
Made It

The rise of Tyler Perry
the most powerful entertainer in Black America
(and what it *really* took to get him there)

Melvin Childs

Touch 1 Media LLC
c/o Book Hub Inc.
903 Pacific Avenue, Suite 207A
Santa Cruz, CA 95060
Phone: 831 466-0145
Email: marketing@book-hub.com

Ordering Information
Quantity sales: Special discounts are available on quantity purchases by corporations, associations, and others. For details, contact the publisher at the address above.

Orders by US trade bookstores and wholesalers:
Please contact Book Hub Distribution at 831 466-0145 or visit www.book-hub.com.

Book design by Stephen Pollard
Cover design by Jamacia Johnson
Front cover by Helga Esteb/Shutterstock.com
Edited by Dawn Daniels
Editorial assistance by Amanda Poulsen Dix

Printed in the United States of America

Library of Congress Control Number: 2011940599

Publisher's Cataloging-In-Publication Data
(Prepared by The Donohue Group, Inc.)

Childs, Melvin.
    Never would have made it : the rise of Tyler Perry, the most powerful entertainer in black America (and what it REALLY took to get him there) / by Melvin Childs.

    p. : ill. ; cm.

    Issued also as an ebook.
    ISBN: 978-0-9847115-0-5 (TC)
    ISBN: 978-0-9847115-1-2 (TP)

    1. Perry, Tyler. 2. African American authors—Biography. 3. African American entertainers—Biography. 4. Motion picture producers and directors—United States—Biography. 5. Television producers and directors--United States--Biography. I. Title.

PN2287.P47 C55 2012
791.4/0973/092   2011940599

ISBN: 978-0-9847115-2-9 eBook

Dedication

For my Nanny, Opal Childs, my living example of what unconditional love is like . . . I love and appreciate you more than I could ever say. You told me Daddy would be proud, I hope you're right.

For Nicholas and Melvin, my greatest joy is watching you grow from boys to men. If I leave you nothing else, at least you have this. Now you don't have to wonder anymore (smile).

Acknowledgements

First, I must thank God above all others for blessing me over and over again even though sometimes I know I haven't deserved it. You have watched over me time and time again even at times when I thought things couldn't be worse . . . and for that, Heavenly Father, I am so thankful.

Secondly, I want to thank my family, without your support none of this would have been possible. You lived this journey with me and I know it was just as hard, if not harder on you, as it was me. Beverly, John, Verdia, Melvin, Nick, Kristie, Kareem, Karrington, Kendall, Rosalinde, Rick, Milas, Lil Ricky, Alex, Nanny, Mama Bea and the entire Ezell family (Y'all know its too many of you to name), I love you all.

Lastly, I would like to thank the members of my extended family who have given me so much help and encouragement: John and Angela, Gary and Angie, Rhonda C., Verb, Scott B., Orel, Pasha, Cliff (lol), James and Nicole, Dus and Shatara, Walt, Melissa, Scott W., Mike A., Nia H., Greg, Stacey, Dawn, Candace, Marva, Francyne, Christine S., Christine M., Greg D., Timothy Allen Smith, Shon and Rebecca and my entire team . . . love y'all.

Special thanks to Thomas and Yvonne, we did it, you both were a pain in the a** the entire way, but I appreciate you more than you can ever know.

Contents

CHAPTER

1

Just Act Normal

She had a cinnamon complexion with long straight hair down to the small of her back. If she had any fat on her, I couldn't see it, and trust me, I could see a lot. If you believe nothing else I am about to say, believe me when I tell you this woman was FINE. In fact, to say she was "fine" doesn't even begin to do her justice. I had seen many attractive women in my time, but this chick looked like she walked straight off the cover of the *Sports Illustrated* Swimsuit Edition, and by the way, she was butt-ass naked.

She was lying on her stomach watching some Spanish-speaking variety show when we walked into the room and, at no time, did she even flinch, much less try to cover herself up. I did my best to play it cool and not stare, thinking my host would quickly usher me into another room to finalize our transaction. I was completely caught off guard when he motioned for me to have a seat in a white leather recliner next to the TV, and left the room.

I stood by the door for a moment, trying to look at least halfway cool. I looked around the room for something, anything I could focus my eyes on and noticed she was burning some kind of apple-scented candle on the dresser. It was weird because you could actually see the fruit inside the candle. I had never seen anything like that where I came from and I wondered to myself what something like that might cost; not that money was an issue. It wasn't . . . not for this guy anyway.

I looked for something else and came up with nothing so when a minute or two had passed, I decided to take my host up on his offer to sit down. Because my assigned seat was next to the television, I found myself face to face with one of the most beautiful women I had ever seen. A woman who, by all accounts, seemed to not give a damn that she had no clothes on. I had given up on any pretense of not staring by this point. The way I figured it, if you leave a 27-year-old man alone in a room with a gorgeous naked woman, you're asking him to stare. You could even argue it would be rude not to. At least that's what I told myself.

While I sat there, "taking in the sights," I wondered what my partners might think if they were sitting here. I smiled to myself at the thought because I knew one of them would've had a fit. Let's just say this wouldn't exactly have been his scene—we'll get more into that a little later. As for my other partner, well, she was more like me in that she was willing to do whatever it took to get this project going so I'm sure she would have sucked it up and dealt with it. As for me, I'd be lying if I told you it was a major problem for me to be sitting in a mansion on Miami Beach, less than five feet from a beautiful naked woman. I had been through a few hard times in my life at that point and, I have to be honest, that wasn't one of them.

Whatever their response might have been really wouldn't have changed anything. It wasn't like we drew straws to decide who was going to make the trip. I was there because I was the only one crazy enough to do it. It really was that simple. And since this was an opportunity none of us could afford to pass up, here I sat.

That was fine by me though. There is a reason it's called a partnership and each of us had a role to play. As long as everybody did their job, we would all be successful. Somebody had to do the dirty work and, seeing as neither of them had the resources or the stomach for this kind of thing, it fell to me. The obvious perks aside, I never particularly enjoyed doing this type of business. I just knew that without it, there was no way we'd be able to keep going. We were literally out of options, so to me, it was worth the risk.

Thinking of the risk brought my mind back to reality. Believe it or not, I had forgotten why I was there. You could say it was the arrogance of youth that allowed me to have such a cavalier attitude about the whole thing. Or you could say my brain was fried from sitting happily immersed in a cloud of fruit-smelling nakedness for too long. Either way, the reality of what I was about to do hadn't set in quite yet, but it was about to.

"Just act normal," said my host, as he walked back into the room and casually tossed a brand new Adidas duffel bag into my lap. The sound of his voice officially snapped me out of what remained of my stupor and I began focusing on the task at hand. I checked the contents of the bag and, seeing everything was in order, zipped it back up and placed it on the floor in front of me. I didn't know exactly what to do next. I think I was subconsciously waiting for him to give me some final instructions, or maybe even give me official permission to leave with the bag. Whatever the case, it was clear he had already moved on with the rest of his life. He poured himself a glass of orange juice from the bar and sat on the bed next to his girl. The three of us sat in awkward silence for a moment until I stood up to leave.

"I better get going," I said as I shifted the bag comfortably onto my shoulder.

"All right my man," he replied coolly. "Have a safe flight."

And with that, I was on my way. I was kind of surprised he didn't have anything to say other than "act normal." He had to know I had never done this type of thing before, so if there was some secret or proven strategy, I would have thought he'd have passed it on. I guess there really was no secret to pass on and, in his mind, he had said everything he needed to. The rest was up to me.

I sat in my rental car for another few minutes, nervously clutching the bag and trying to determine if I was really going to go through with this. It didn't take me long to realize there was no turning back. I had risked everything to make this happen and there were too many people counting on me for me to walk away now. I had to see this through no matter what the cost.

The next part of the trip seemed fairly mundane. I had a 5 o'clock flight to Atlanta so I planned to be at Miami International by 3:30 in the afternoon. I was a frequent flyer in those days and took great pride in knowing the exact itinerary for my particular needs on any given trip. That's why I chose a Tuesday morning for the meeting. I knew the crowds would be small and, as long as I avoided rush hour, traffic would be minimal. It seemed like a perfect plan. It wasn't until I arrived at the airport that I realized my mistake.

The whole damn place was like a ghost town. There were maybe five people in the security line and two more waiting at the ticket counter. Everyone seemed to be going about their business without incident and so I figured all I would have to do is fit in. The problem was there were more employees in the concourse than customers and they all seemed bored enough to want to do their jobs. I knew right away this was not good for me.

"Just act normal." The words played over and over in my head as I found myself subconsciously walking very slowly towards the security checkpoint. This was a bad idea. No, it was a HORRIBLE idea. We clearly hadn't thought this through.

"May I help you?"

I just about jumped out of my skin as I turned to see a pleasant looking, middle-aged Latin lady smiling up at me. I noticed she was wearing a uniform, and she must have noticed the look of sheer terror on my face as she immediately apologized.

"I'm sorry, did I startle you?" she asked gently. "I thought you might need some help finding your gate."

I looked at her blankly and tried to muster up some sort of smile. I had no idea what I was supposed to say to her but I had to think of something quick.

"Umm, no. I was just umm; I was looking for my partner." I lied, trying to calm myself down. "Oh, there he is over there,"

I said quickly then unceremoniously changed direction and walked toward a group of three middle aged white men checking their bags with an agent. The way I acted I'm surprised that lady didn't call the cops on my ass right then. She must have just thought I was on something; we were in Miami after all. Or maybe she figured I was some kind of weirdo. Whatever the case, I had to get out of this airport before things got any worse.

As I walked away, I resisted the temptation to look back. I felt the eyes of the entire Miami International security apparatus were directed solely at me so I couldn't afford to draw any more attention to myself. If that wasn't bad enough, my heart was beating so hard I'm sure anyone standing close enough would have been able to hear it. I noticed I was starting to sweat so I stopped at the flight information board to try to compose myself. "Just act normal" was quickly replaced by "what the hell was I thinking" as the song playing on an infinite loop inside my brain. I always knew the end of this trip could take countless forms. I now realized they all led me to the same place—jail. Well, to be honest, there was another option, but I didn't even want to think about that right now.

I sucked it up and moved toward the security line, trying to focus on my team in Atlanta and my family back in Oklahoma City. I knew what it would mean to them if I could pull this off and the last thing I wanted was to let any of them down. As much as we'd been through together and as hard as we worked to get to this point, we all knew none of it would matter if I didn't get this package back to Atlanta.

The year was 1998 and all I can say is, thank God it was before September 11 because, looking back, I was acting anything but normal. Under today's rules, they'd have locked me up and strip-searched me in thirty seconds. The whole thing seemed like an out of body experience, and the closer I got to going through the scanner, the slower things around me seemed to move. My moment of truth was about to arrive and it was becoming increasingly clear with every step that I was not ready for whatever was about to happen. My mind raced for something, anything I could say, but I kept coming up blank. The truth is,there simply wasn't an answer for the most obvious question sure to come from the cackle of suddenly diligent security agents invading my personal space at the moment.

"Sir, why do you have a hundred thousand dollars in cash in your carry-on?"

All I could think was, "Just act normal."

＊　　＊　　＊

The takeoff seemed exceptionally smooth which probably had a little something to do with my being physically on the plane without handcuffs. I was offered a free upgrade to first class and, given my stressful ordeal getting through security, I felt obligated to treat myself to a glass of champagne. As the flight reached altitude, I reclined my seat and couldn't help but smile. It was finally happening. All of a sudden, the picture began to crystallize for me in a way that was a little overwhelming.

Of the three partners on the project, I was the only one with any kind of regular income. My partner, Nia Hill, was very well connected in the city of Atlanta and was instrumental in putting the pieces together from the beginning. I can honestly say none of this would have happened without her but she wasn't exactly making big money at the time. The financial burden of getting this done all fell on me and I had spent the better part of a year going broke trying to keep the project afloat. As broke as I was though, I was much better off than either one of them and that's what made this moment so special.

From the beginning, none of us had a clue what the hell we were doing. We just knew we had a product we believed in so we literally put everything we had into it. Unfortunately, as the three of us learned very clearly, that wasn't going to be enough. All the hard work, talent and sacrifice in the world don't mean a damn thing without the means to move forward. Now we had them . . . in my carry on.

"Sir, would you like a refill?" said the flight attendant as she offered me more champagne.

"Absolutely," I replied, handing her my fancy plastic champagne glass. I sat back into my leather seat and decided to try to take a nap. The sheer sense of relief I felt upon takeoff was quickly being replaced by fatigue. As I started to close my eyes, the intercom came on with an announcement, "Ladies and gentlemen, the captain has turned on the fasten seatbelt sign. Please return to your seats and be sure your seatbelt is securely fastened as we will likely experience some turbulence on our way to Atlanta." The mention of turbulence immediately turned my thoughts to our third partner on this project.

If Nia and I had risked our life savings, he had already LOST everything he had trying to make this happen. And I'm not just talking about money. I don't want to minimize what we had invested, but there was no question that his life literally depended on the success of this project. He could be a handful at times, but then again, what artist wasn't? The important thing was he was talented and unquestionably committed to making this work. I believed in him and his talent from the start. So much so that I supported him financially for months as we tried to find a way to remount his show. Food, hotels, spending money, you name it.

I didn't mind though. I considered him a friend and lord knows he needed the help. He was flat-ass broke when I met him and since he had already given up everything he had to get the project this far, I was just doing what I could to keep things going. It was almost unreal to think about how far he had come since we first met, and honestly, I couldn't have been happier for him, especially now that he was going to get his shot. What I had in my carry-on was going to mean a lot to Nia and me, there was no question about that, but for Tyler Perry, we were literally about to change his life.

CHAPTER

2

Setting the Record Straight

"Where's Melvin Childs at? Y'all bring up the house lights, where's Melvin Childs?" bellowed the booming voice from the stage.

I was there as much out of curiosity as anything else. It was 2007 and I heard on the radio that Tyler was bringing his latest show, "Madea Goes to Jail," to Oklahoma City. I hadn't seen or spoken to him in years so I guess a part of me just wanted to see what he was up to. Not that it was any kind of secret what the man had been doing. He was a full on celebrity by this point so a quick internet search would have told me everything I needed to know about the life of Tyler Perry, or at least that's what he would have you believe.

In that sense, Tyler isn't all that different from many other celebrities. One of the many perks of fame is that you get to rewrite whatever your personal story was before you became somebody. Your PR machine controls everything about your personal life once you hit it big. And the bigger you get, the larger the machine you need to put in place to justify your elevated status. It's all about managing how you come across to people, and the story of how you made it is a big piece of that.

All celebrities protect this "back-story" because it helps them appear relatable to their audience. Being relatable is the key to being likable, and being likable is the key to making money. No star, especially one with as loyal a following as Tyler Perry, can afford to lose touch with their core audience. They need to be "one of us" if they expect us to support them and Tyler's back-story is designed to make you feel as though through faith and hard work, you too can achieve what he has.

Unfortunately that's not the way it works. I know how that sounds, but hold on Saints. Don't give up on me yet. I'll explain that one later.

So as I sat and watched Tyler doing his thing that night, I couldn't help but think about what his back-story would be like if I had written it. Having been as close to the action as I was at one point, I always thought I had an interesting story to tell. I just never had any real motivation to tell it. What happened seemed like a lifetime ago and everyone had moved on to bigger, if not better, things.

Still, I wondered what people might say if they ever heard the real story of how Tyler made it big. To be honest, I wasn't sure that Tyler himself could remember what happened back then. He answered that question for me by calling me out by name during the curtain call of his performance.

He knew I was there because I stopped by the theater earlier that afternoon. I wanted to see for myself how the operation had grown since the early days when it was basically just him stuffing everything he owned into the back seat of his red BMW. Since I knew the building managers, I had no problem getting back stage where I ran into Chris Locklear, the stage manager. I personally hired Chris ten years earlier and remembered him to be a good dude. We caught up for a few minutes while he showed me around. I got to look at the set and the lighting, and I have to admit, I was very impressed. Not that I was all that surprised. I didn't have much good to say about any of the people Tyler now had running things for him, one person in particular, but I could honestly say that they knew their business.

It was the middle of the afternoon, and I had some things to do before the show, so I was about to get going when I asked Chris where Tyler was.

"Awww, you know how he is Melvin," he said with a knowing smile. "Lemme tell him you here before I bring you back to his dressing room."

Chris went to talk to Tyler, leaving me alone in the green room to collect my thoughts. Even though so much time had gone by, I wasn't the least bit nervous or tense about seeing him. A lot of bad shit went down but most of it had very little to do with Tyler. Nia and I got screwed because we didn't know enough about the business to prevent it from happening, simple as that. Now you could say Tyler was complicit in much of it by allowing it to happen but, in fairness, there is no way he was the mastermind behind anything. He knew even less about the business than we did. He damn sure didn't know enough to develop the plan himself. That was entirely someone else's doing.

"He's getting his makeup on right now," said Chris as he came back into the room. "He said he'll get with you after the show." I knew the routine well enough to know "after the show" meant I was to come back stage and mingle with the masses while waiting patiently for an audience with the man himself. I'm sure he knew me well enough to know that wasn't gonna happen.

That was cool with me. After everything we'd been through, it would have been weird to not at least try to say hello, especially since we were less than fifty feet from each other at the time. The truth is I'm not all that sure we had anything to talk about. I guess he felt the same and I didn't take it personally.

See, Tyler and I never really had any kind of major falling out. Of course there were disagreements, some of them pretty heated, but that is to be expected when you've got a group of twenty-somethings out there on the road trying to get something that had never been done before off the ground. And make no mistake about it, what we were producing had not been seen before in the black community. Don't get me wrong, gospel plays had been around forever. It's just that what we created was something beyond the typical nonsense presented on the so-called Chitlin Circuit back then. We knew we had something special, and we fought tooth and nail to get it out there.

Working with that kind of passion is bound to cause conflict and, yes, we butted heads more than a few times. Through it all though, we never lost focus on the big picture. We knew if we could find a way to get the show up and in front of the right audience, we could be successful. Was it easy? No, of course not, but we leaned on each other and that, as much as anything else, is what made it worthwhile. To me, there's nothing more rewarding than being able to share success with the very people who were side-by-side with me during the bad times. I've learned that not everybody feels that way.

"Melvin Childs," he said dramatically as I stood up from my seat in the second row. The performance was finished and, as is his custom, Tyler was on stage addressing the audience. I had no idea he would call me out by name, and I had even less idea what he was about to say. "Not many people know this, but Melvin here was my very first promoter until he decided to leave me for bigger and better things. How's that workin' out for ya?" he asked sarcastically as he folded his arms in front of him and flashed his most charismatic smile. He got the laugh he was going for as I sat back down. The fact that it was at my expense didn't bother me nearly as much as the characterization of my role as merely a promoter.

The drive home was quiet. My seven year old son was with me and as I looked over at him dozing off in the passenger seat, I couldn't help but feel like a failure. The emotion I felt in that moment was raw and the entire weight of those years came down on me all at once. It's a significant moment in any young man's life when he sees his father cry for the first time. I was lucky little Melvin was sleeping so that I wouldn't have to explain my tears. Not these tears, not like this.

Seeing Tyler on that stage and having him mock me in front of my son the way he did was incredibly insulting. What would it have cost him to be gracious? What would he have sacrificed to simply say thank you for all I had done? And believe me, I did a LOT. I sacrificed more than he could possibly know to launch his career and now he was acting as if my being a part of his story would somehow diminish what he had accomplished. It would have been one thing to just ignore me and pretend I wasn't there. I could have accepted that as just an ego driven slight. But to spit in my face like that . . . and laugh about it?! No, this was beyond just insulting. The anger was building but I had nowhere to vent it. All I could do was clench the steering wheel and swallow my pride as I made my way through town to my home.

It was a long ride home that night. A quiet ride. There were so many things I wanted to say. So many things I wished I had done differently but life doesn't come with a time machine. We can't go back, as much as we sometimes wish we could. We have to accept the past, learn from it and move forward. For the most part, I think I've done exactly that. I worked hard to get beyond the bitterness and anger and honestly, I thought I had; at least until that night.

That night was a turning point for me. Until that night, I had defended Tyler to anyone close enough to me to know the true story. I'm talking about the truth; not the spin he puts out on Oprah or the half-truth you can read on his website. I'm talking about the real story of how he went from being a failed playwright performing in churches for fifty people, to being Tyler Perry. I'm talking about the time in the beginning when I had lost my job and would take money from my wife and send it to Tyler to help pay his bills. I know what happened because I was there and, what's more important, Tyler knows I was there.

His words, "Melvin here was my first promoter," rolled around in my mind as I got closer and closer to home.

The more I thought about it, the more it started to piss me off. Was I just a promoter when you came to me for a loan because you didn't have the money to pay your cast? Was I just a promoter when you called me to borrow money to buy food or when I personally paid for the hotel you were living in while you were supposedly homeless? Maybe I was and if that's the case, then so be it. But guess what? Regardless of what he wants to call me, I was there. And because I was there, I also have a story to tell.

This is a behind-the-scenes look at how Tyler Perry became Tyler Perry. And I can tell this story because it's mine. These are not rumors or things I heard from anonymous sources. These are things I saw, things I did and conversations I had. Everything I am about to say happened. I know it. And Tyler knows it.

Time to set the record straight . . .

CHAPTER

3

Hello Arthur

Arthur Primas has been Tyler Perry's lead promoter, theatrical producer and all around right hand man for the better part of thirteen years. As a result, he is an extremely wealthy man. He's also a very private person, which is why most of you have probably never heard his name.

Back in the day, before anyone had ever heard of Tyler Perry, Arthur was an event planner for the Myriad Convention Center in Oklahoma City until he was fired for some transgression or another. I don't know the exact details, only what I read online when I was trying to find details about a lawsuit he filed, and lost, against the city. I do know Arthur, quite well in fact, and nothing would surprise me where he is concerned.

I hadn't officially met him while he was working at the Myriad, but I definitely knew who he was. Oklahoma City is small with a relatively small black community so everyone in town tends to at least know of one another. Additionally, I was a sales representative for KVSP, the only black radio station in the area. Since the Myriad was considered THE place in town to host major concerts and events, any sales rep worth a penny would have been familiar with their event coordinators.

None of that mattered much to me personally though. Because we were, literally, the only radio station in the city with a mainstream urban format, which is just a fancy way of saying we played black music and catered to a predominantly black audience. I didn't have to spend much time chasing down contacts. Whenever a black artist came to town, their promoters had no choice but to come to us to advertise, and I just happened to be the man those promoters bought their radio spots from.

The money was decent but I was more concerned with the swag I developed by being the man all these big time promoters and artists had to come to.

Putting on an R-Kelly concert at the civic center?

Call Melvin Childs.

Wanna promote Keith Sweat at the Zoo Amphitheater?

Call Melvin Childs.

Boyz To Men at the Myriad?

Call Melvin Childs.

Toni Braxton, En Vogue, Johnny Gill, you name it. All the major black artists of that era came through Oklahoma City at one point or another and all of their promoters had to come to me. It wasn't like I was the only sales rep at the station. I was just the one who had a rapport with the promoters, so I was the one they wanted to deal with. Now if there is such a thing as a golden age of the promotions game, the nineties might have been it. The economy was booming, people had money to spend and they seemed very willing to spend it on entertainment.

Concert and play tickets consistently sold very well and even though not every show coming through town sold out, it was clear that if you had the right talent, and an adequate budget for advertising, you had a chance to be successful, and by successful I mean you could make money.

It seemed like everybody was getting paid back then. The venues, the promoters, the talent, the radio stations, the sales reps—we were all making money hand over fist and, under those circumstances, it's fairly easy to make friends with the people you're doing business with. That's how I came to know David Brooks.

David was a local club owner but you would never know it to look at him. He's a light skinned black dude with a shaved head, full beard and absolutely no flash to him whatsoever. When I say no flash I mean he buys his clothes at Wal-Mart, drives a raggedy car and probably still has his lunch money from grade school. Women always seemed to like him though. He's got a little of that Shemar Moore kind of thing happening. Plus, he's a former bodybuilder standing a little less than six feet tall at about two hundred pounds of solid muscle.

David's always been a smart dude; one of the smartest guys I know. He saw no reason to waste money trying to impress anybody. If you saw him walking down the street, you wouldn't get the impression he owned a nightclub or anything else for that matter. Hell, if you saw the car he drove, you'd probably think he was unemployed and living in his mom's basement. He is a low profile kind of dude, so flossing has no appeal to him; which probably explains why he always seems to have money.

Of course I didn't know any of that when we first met. When I met David, he was just another sad-sack club owner who seemed to be missing out on the entertainment boom happening all around him. In other words, he was getting his ass kicked running his club and couldn't figure out why. When I took a look at the kind of promotion he was doing and saw that he was playing techno music, trying, unsuccessfully, to attract a mixed crowd, I advised him to switch formats and cater to the kind of urban, black audience he could reach by advertising on KVSP. He quickly agreed and had me put together an ad package for him. I set up a few promotions at the station and, in a short time, his business was booming. It took less than two months for him to go from losing thousands of dollars a week to making real money, and because I played such a major role in getting things rolling, he trusted just about everything I had to say when it came to business. He had no reason not to.

To this day David is one of my closest friends, but it took some time for that to develop. Back then I viewed my relationship with him the same way I viewed my so-called friendships with any of the people I met through the station. I saw them all as potential resources. Yes, I was doing well selling advertising but I had my eyes on bigger things. I saw the kind of money the promoters were making and, to put it bluntly, I wanted in.

I was young and clueless at the time, but I was still smart enough to realize that what you knew mattered a lot less in this business than who you knew. If I wanted to get into the game in any kind of real way, I would need money, and David and my other "friends" were the people who had it. For me to have the chance to do anything other than what I was already doing, I would have to make a conscious effort to keep those guys close.

So that's what I did. In a handful of cases, those relationships moved beyond the professional level and developed into more personal friendships. David is one of those examples, and Arthur Primas was another. In fact, as close as David and I would eventually become, our friendship paled in comparison to how close I was with Arthur. If David was a best friend, Arthur was more like family.

Things continued to go well at work. The station was making so much money that the owner opened up another radio station in Tulsa, about an hour east of Oklahoma City. The format would be similar to ours at KVSP so, naturally, I was made the lead rep there as well. Not only did this mean more money, but now I could build my network to include an even broader area. Keep in mind this was the early nineties and there really was no internet or any other kind of alternative marketing available to promoters. Radio and TV was it and I already controlled black radio in Oklahoma City. Adding Tulsa to the mix made me even more confident that the time was coming for me to branch off into other things.

After getting fired from the Myriad, Arthur hooked up with Al Wash, who was the major promoter of gospel plays touring the so-called Chitlin Circuit. The Chitlin' Circuit was the nickname given to a group of cities and venues, primarily in the South, that welcomed black shows. The nickname dated back to the sixties in the pre-segregation era, but the concept lived on well into the nineties and beyond. Oklahoma City and Tulsa were two of the primary stops on the Chitlin Circuit at that time so Arthur and Al would periodically bring productions into my territory. When they did, of course, they would have to buy advertising from me.

Looking back on it, I'm not sure if Arthur worked for Al Wash or with him. I just knew they worked together and Arthur would periodically come down to the station to discuss his promotion needs. He's short for a man at about five-six but, while he's far from a bodybuilder, he is powerfully built. He was in his fifties when we met but still carried himself with an athlete's bearing. Which is to say, he didn't move around like an old man. In fact, for years he was a high school basketball referee, which definitely suited his personality.

Arthur Primas is a lot of things but humble is not one of them. He wasn't then, and he isn't today. The next time Arthur admits he is wrong about something will probably be the first time, and he has no problem letting anyone know how smart he is. Especially yours truly.

"Melvin Childs you don't know what the hell you talking about." He would say with a level of self-assuredness unbefitting any mere mortal. If I ever dared disagree with him it was always "Alright Melvin Childs, I done told you. Don't come to me when you done got your ass kicked."

That was Arthur. He considered himself to be THE authority on all things related to the promotions business, and he was constantly setting me straight, even when I didn't want his opinion.

In the beginning, our relationship was mostly professional. Like any of my other clients back then, I made the extra effort to keep things friendly but Arthur is a very straight forward kind of guy. As far as he was concerned, he was there to buy advertising. I, of course, was there to sell it. Doesn't get any simpler than that. And things would have stayed simple if that's all our relationship had ever been about. But I wanted in on the action and, as time went on, I became convinced that Arthur Primas would be my ticket to the party.

He began to frequent the station more often so I was eventually able to get him to loosen up and that's when we started to develop a rapport.

"How you doin' Melvin Childs?" he said loudly as he barreled his way into the station back office. "You ready to make me some money?"

"Have I ever let you down?"

"Well let's get to it young man!" he said with a smile. "Let's go get this paper."

That's the thing about Arthur. As abrasive and unapproachable as he can be, he can also be very personable when he wants to. You just need to work your way into his inner circle before you get to see that side of him.

"Hey, let me ask you something," I said as we were wrapping up a meeting. "How does this gospel play thing work?"

"What you mean 'how does it work?'"

"I mean, how much money can y'all make with one of these things?"

"C'mon Melvin Childs, you can do that math by yourself. There are eight shows in a standard week. Now if you can do a thousand seats per show at thirty-five dollars a pop . . . fool you don't need a calculator to see you done got paid AND you ain't even selling out the house!"

I have to admit I was blown away by the numbers. That was thirty grand per show after building expenses, and he wasn't even talking about the most popular ones. The more popular shows were definitely selling out several shows per week and I knew the houses they were playing sat close to two thousand people. "So you're telling me y'all can gross over two hundred fifty-thousand dollars in a week?"

"I'm telling you if you have the right show in the right markets, you can do more than that."

I was shocked when he broke it down to me. Call it greed or ambition or whatever you want but I knew that if people were out there making that kind of money, I had to get a piece of that. Why was I wasting my time selling radio spots when the real money was in promoting one of these shows? I knew immediately what I needed to do.

I asked Arthur about a million more questions, and he seemed to have a million and one answers. "The key is controlling your expenses," he would say with the authority of someone who had learned this particular lesson the hard way. "You GOT to keep them expenses low if you want to make money out there on the road."

Talking to him, I couldn't help but feel like he knew everything there was to know about the promotions business. Not only that, he seemed to know everyone of any importance in the game. The more he told me, the more I wanted to know. I soaked up the information like a sponge and sought his advice even more. I was afraid I might alienate him by asking so many questions constantly, but he was always very receptive and brutally honest.

This was comforting, in an odd way, because I didn't have very many people in my life willing to challenge me in those days. My father passed away when I was twenty-two so I had never had an opportunity to have any kind of adult relationship with him. Consequently, when I started getting to know Arthur, he began to fill that void. I, of course, didn't realize any of this at the time. I just figured we had some things in common and so we were hitting it off. Had I been more self-aware, I could have probably prevented a lot of what would eventually happen. The problem was I was doing very well for myself so I had no sense of anything missing in my life besides money. I figured if I could get myself, paid in a major way, I would be set so that's all I focused on. The fact that Arthur was so willing to help influenced me to drop my guard even further until, eventually, he became someone I looked up to. I respected him not only for what he knew, but for the way he so readily shared what he knew with me. The fact that he cared enough to put me in my place from time to time convinced me even more that this was someone I could trust. I felt like he wasn't just telling me what I wanted to hear. And that made me feel like he had my best interest at heart.

My friendship with Arthur had given me something I never even knew I was missing and, in return, he knew that he would always be able to count on me. I started turning to him more often and our conversations became increasingly personal. Eventually he invited me over to his home where I met his wife, Brenda, and both of his kids. Of course I continued asking him questions about certain promotions and seeking his advice on things related to the business, but I also felt like we had developed a significant, personal friendship. Over time, I found myself wanting not only his advice, but his approval. Keep in mind, Arthur is almost twenty years older than me so it's only natural that, as we grew closer, I would see him as a paternal figure. The connection I felt with him and his family had become very real to me and I began to look out for them like they were my own. I didn't have a lot, but whatever I had was theirs if they needed it.

"Hey Melvin Childs, how you doin?" he said as I answered the phone in my office one afternoon.

"What's up Arthur? Where you at?"

"Hey listen," he said, ignoring my question. "I need you to run by the house and give Brenda fifteen hundred for me. Can you do that? I'll get you back when I get home."

"Don't worry about it. I got you."

It wasn't unusual for Arthur to call me from out on the road somewhere and ask me stop by the house and give Brenda a couple thousand dollars until he got back to town. Don't get me wrong, a few grand was, and is, a lot of money to me. But I never once hesitated when he asked. I promise you, every time he called; I made it my business to be there for him. Not out of obligation or because I ever expected anything in return. Arthur was my dawg, and I was just doing what I was supposed to do. And besides, I knew he would have done the same for me if the tables were ever turned.

As I continued to turn to him for advice, I grew increasingly confident that I was ready to do a promotion of my own. A gospel play was still a little out of my reach so I focused on making some extra cash by promoting some smaller shows on my own. I started off with small R&B acts like Howard Hewitt, did some jazz shows, a few night club acts, etc. Over time I built a nice little side business in and around Oklahoma City and Tulsa.

This did not please my boss. He was ticked off that I was doing anything besides selling advertising for his radio stations so he started closely monitoring my time at work. He wanted to know what time I came in and when I went home, how long I took for lunch, how many client calls I made per day, etc. He was determined to find something, anything, which would give him cause to fire me.

As for me? I wasn't the least bit concerned with any of that nonsense. Don't get me wrong, I showed up to work on time and continued to do my job. It's just that my focus was somewhere else. I was starting to make headway as a promoter so the radio job became more like a small, entry-level position that was a steppingstone for me. I needed to move beyond that to get where I wanted and so the prospect of losing the gig didn't really scare me. A part of me probably wished I would get fired so that I could focus solely on my promotions business. I understand now why they say you should be careful what you wish for.

Arthur counseled me on which acts to bring into town and which venues made the most sense. In a short time, I was bringing home an average of five thousand dollars per show, and, with Arthur's help, had never lost money on a promotion. Now, as promoters go, I was definitely small time, but I was absolutely making money. That's what was so strange about Arthur's situation.

Even with all of his knowledge and experience, he was flat broke. And no, he wasn't like David, keeping his financial status low key. Arthur was living paycheck to paycheck at best, and his paychecks weren't regular. He was constantly borrowing money, lived in a raggedy old house on a bad side of town and drove around in a banged up, faded blue Volvo with no air conditioning. The man had connections and ambition for days, but the one thing he didn't seem to have was money and, to be honest, this started to affect my perception of him a little bit.

If that sounds arrogant, I have to own up to it. Keep in mind I was in my twenties and dealing with A-list artists and promoters on a regular basis. It would have been difficult for any young man to keep his perspective under those circumstances. I don't think I went too far with it, but I definitely developed a big head based on the few successes I had early on. And while Arthur was definitely my closest friend in the business, he was far from my only one.

As long as I had my job at the station, the promoters knew it was in their best interest to keep me in their inner circle. Could they have gone elsewhere to buy their ads? Yeah absolutely. But here is the dirty little secret of radio advertising; radio spots don't sell tickets. What sells tickets is the promotion done by the station in support of your event. The successful promoters all know this, so they make it their business to have someone inside the station working on their team, making sure the jocks are mentioning their event, doing ticket giveaways— all the things required to get butts in seats at their events. At my stations, I was their man.

Of course I knew they needed me so my ego only got bigger. You couldn't tell me a thing because, as much as Arthur tried to put me in my place, I seriously thought I had the world figured out. Then, when I was able to make money doing the promotion thing and he obviously wasn't, I naturally began to assume I knew as much as he did, and maybe even a thing or two more. I never quite lost respect for him, per se. I just figured the game had kind of passed him by and that it was time for the next generation to step up to the plate. Personally, I felt I was more than ready for the challenge.

Everything else aside, Arthur was a hustler and that's one of the many things I admired about him. He always seemed to be working an angle, trying to beat the system. I was too young and wrapped up in my own thing to recognize it at the time, but Arthur is an extreme opportunist. The fact that he didn't have money probably just meant he was waiting for the next opportunity and, for someone like him, there would always be another opportunity.

Arthur also has one very special talent. He is a charismatic dude who can earn your trust and use it to manipulate any situation to his advantage. There's a part of me that likes to think I suspected this about him even back then and, in a way, I guess I did. I just didn't care. No man is perfect and whatever faults he had, I just accepted him for who he was because, for me, he was like a father.

Regardless of what he might have done to anybody else, I KNEW there was no way in the world he would ever steal from me. We were way too close for that. It would take me years to figure out exactly how wrong I was.

CHAPTER

4

We Can Do This

The formula for a gospel play:

1) Son is a Gang-banger (Father ain't around)
2) Grandmamma prays for her grandson (who also sells drugs)
3) Somebody dies
4) Whole family prays some more
5) Gang-banging, dope-dealing, fatherless grandson gets saved
6) Everybody gives God the glory
7) The end

That's what was being offered on the gospel play circuit back then. Add in the fact that the marketing made these shows feel like you were going to a revival at your local church and I'm pretty sure single, twenty-six year old males were not a part of their core demographic.

That's what made Tyler's stuff so appealing to me. He didn't adhere to that tired formula and created something that felt more real. I know he has a ton of detractors who say his shows amount to little more than the same old tired exploitation of negative stereotypes that have been around since Stepin Fetchit. But I challenge anyone to look back at what was on the chitlin circuit prior to Tyler blowing up and find something that compares.

Tyler Perry deserves credit for what he created because it truly changed the game in terms of how gospel plays were produced and perceived. What he does not deserve the credit for is taking what he had created from an empty church in Montgomery Alabama to a sold out run at the House of Blues in Atlanta.

Question: "If a tree falls in a forest and no one is around to hear it, does it make a sound?"

Answer: "Nobody cares."

That was Tyler back then. He had talent, there is no question, but since nobody was there to see it, nobody cared, and that's the point. He was every bit as talented then as he is today. So what changed? He got some help. That's the big revelation. He did not go from an obscure unknown talent in Alabama, and Saint Louis for that matter too, to become the toast of Atlanta all by himself, while living out of his car. It took a lot of hard work, faith, and CASH to get him to the House of Blues. That sold out run is where the Tyler Perry, as we know him today, was born, but that's not where he began.

Many of those pre-Tyler Perry productions came through Oklahoma City and for a long time, even though I was curious and had countless conversations with Arthur about how it all worked, I never took the time to go see one. The closest I came was managing the promotions of a few of the bigger productions at the radio station. Working on the advertising end, it didn't take me very long to figure out I had no interest in what they were offering.

What did interest me was money and I used to see, first hand, the kind of money these productions spent on advertising. Somebody had to be making some serious bank for them to have the advertising budgets they had. Eventually my curiosity got the better of me, and I decided to see for myself what went on at one of these shows. I promised myself I would go see the next major production that visited Tulsa or Oklahoma City.

My opportunity came when I worked on a promotion involving Melba Moore. She was starring in a play titled 'Mama I'm Sorry' showing at the Brady Theater in Tulsa.

Michael Matthews who, according to Arthur, was a fairly big name on the gospel play circuit wrote the play. Melba was coming in to do an interview and I figured I'd stick around to see what the show was about. If it seemed even halfway interesting, I would go check it out that night.

Well, it didn't seem even halfway interesting. In fact, my perception from the interview was that it would be a hot, ghetto mess. Aside from Melba, the cast was made up of virtual nobodies and the whole thing had kind of a thrown together feel to it. I didn't see any way possible the quality of this production could be anything but horrible. Still, they were spending a ton on advertising so I stayed true to my word and picked up some tickets. I had no plans that night and it's not like I had to travel very far. Who knows, maybe it would be better than I thought—wrong.

Everything I initially thought was true. It was poorly written, poorly acted and the set looked like something I threw together in my backyard. Here's the thing though . . . there were more than seventeen hundred people in that audience and, as far as I could tell, there was only one dissatisfied customer . . . me.

At twenty-five dollars per ticket they had grossed over forty-thousand dollars in one night. Average that over an eight show week and you are looking at more than three hundred thousand dollars gross per week. Three hundred thousand dollars for that mess of a show? I knew then and there I had to get into this business.

About a week or so later, I received a call from one of my associates in Atlanta. Her name was Nia Hill and, to be honest, she was more of a personal acquaintance than an actual business associate. We knew each other from my job at the station and from me doing my side thing as a promoter. She was constantly pitching Atlanta-based acts for me to bring to Oklahoma City and, even though we never did a deal together, she called often enough that we became friendly. I can't say we were friends at that point because we had never met in person. Our entire relationship was built over the phone and that was primarily based on her calling me at the station to see if we could do some type of promotion together. I got the sense, both from the frequency of her calls and by how hard she pushed some of these acts, that she needed the money, and that she was a hustler. I guess I respected her tenacity so I always had her in the back of my mind as someone to hook up if I ever had any kind of business to throw her way.

That day she was going on and on about some act she wanted me to bring to town when, all of a sudden, it hit me. "Nia," I interrupted her mid-sentence. "Do you know anybody who wrote a play?"

"A what?" she responded, clearly annoyed at being interrupted.

"A play, a gospel play. Do you know anybody who wrote one?"

"Not off the top of my head, no. Why?"

"I want to promote one here in Oklahoma City. If you come across anybody with a good one let me know."

"OK, but what about this other thing I was . . ."

"Nia, I aint trying to hear all that." I said, interrupting her again. "Find me a playwright I can work with, and I'll put you in the deal." Those were the magic words for Nia. She now knew she would get a piece of the action if she found me somebody with a play I could work with.

She told me again that she didn't know anyone off hand, but said she would ask around and let me know. I had no doubt she would find me somebody. Like I said, she was a hustler and if there was a playwright to be found in the city of Atlanta, Nia would find him for me.

I didn't give it much thought after that initial conversation. Keep in mind my desire to get into the play business had nothing to do with any love of theater or commitment to the arts. I hated everything I had ever seen that even resembled a play, gospel or otherwise. For me, it was strictly about making money so I didn't come at this from the perspective of an artist looking to be discovered. I looked at it like a businessman in search of the right business opportunity. And as any decent businessman knows, the right opportunity means nothing if you don't have the resources in place to take advantage of it. Understanding this, my next call was to my old friend, David Brooks.

David's club had been doing exceptionally well, so I knew the money wouldn't be a huge issue for him. What might be a concern was the fact that we had become legitimate friends by that time and, knowing David, he would probably be a little hesitant to get into business with a friend. I didn't think our friendship would be a deal breaker, but you never know so I figured I better feel him out right away. That way I would know, up front, if I needed to look elsewhere for funding.

As it turned out, David had no issues or concerns whatsoever. He had made so much money with me working on his club promotion that he was very willing to listen to just about anything I had to say when it came to business. Plus, he had already backed me on a few small promotions that always made his money back plus some profit. Yes, the amount of money I was talking about this time was larger than anything he had fronted me before. But as far as David Brooks was concerned, if I said it was going to make money, it was going to make money. So when I broke down how I saw this play thing working out, he was all in.

Now that I had the funding in place, there really was nothing to do but wait. I thought about calling Arthur to get his thoughts, but ultimately decided to wait until I had something concrete to discuss. I had learned to be a little cautious around Arthur when there was money to be spent. Not that I was worried about him ripping me off or anything like that, but pointing Arthur Primas in the direction of available cash is kind of like putting a drop of blood in a pool of hungry sharks. Eventually his instincts would take over and he wouldn't be able to stop himself until every available dime he could grab for himself was gone, regardless of who lost what in the process.

I saw this first hand when I told Arthur about a group of guys who had called the station from California wanting to be promoters. Apparently one of them had received a huge settlement from some kind of accident and wanted to get into the promotions game. This happened all the time back then and, once I was sure they had money, I would always file their contact info away as potential resources for one of my projects. These particular guys were originally pitching some hip-hop act from Los Angeles but I steered them in the direction of a project I wanted to do centered around the homecoming weekend at Langston University, a predominantly black university located just 45 miles north of Oklahoma City.

They seemed interested and when I told Arthur about them, he immediately began selling me on this oldies show he had just produced with Al Wash starring the Chi-Lites, the Manhattans, Enchantment, and Ray-Goodman and Brown. The show had just come off some kind of tour so the ramp up time would be minimal. He went on and on about how great it was and how we would make a killing if I could get these guys to put up the money. Now I was only interested in the Langston home coming date, but in order for it to make sense financially, my friends from California would have to finance a mini tour with dates in other cities. To me, it seemed like a good deal so I sold them on financing this tour that Arthur would produce. Unfortunately, the whole thing was a mess from day one.

I don't know if it was a problem with the marketing or what, but from the first show we were getting killed at least according to Arthur. The guys who put up the money trusted me to look out for them so they never came out to see what was going on for themselves. And since Arthur was out on the road with the show, running things, I saw no need for me to be out there too. Besides, I was really only concerned with my Langston promotion so I spent all my time focusing on that.

Leaving everything in Arthur's hands meant all we had to go on at the end of the week was a report listing of what we made and how much we spent. The report was horrible and, to make matters worse, the Chi-Lites, who were the headliners, dropped off the tour.

"What do you mean there ain't no Chi-Lites?!" I said in a panic.

"I got in an argument with Marshall, one of the original Chi-Lites and now I too got to teach his ass a lesson." He responded.

"Arthur, do you know how much advertising I've done in Oklahoma City promoting the fucking Chi-Lites as the headline act?!"

"Calm down Melvin Childs." he said, turning on the charm. "The audience won't even know they ain't there."

"They're the fucking headliners!"

"Watch, you'll see."

I was amazed, and a little annoyed, at how unfazed he was by the whole thing. To be honest, I had no real choice but to trust him though. I couldn't afford, financially, to turn back and the promotion was going very well, except for the fact we were promoting an act that, apparently, wasn't going to be there.

As it turned out, Arthur was right. Because of the way the show was produced the audience never even knew the Chi-Lites weren't there and the Langston promotion went very well. I came out of that event with close to fifteen thousand dollars so I was obviously very happy with the way things turned out for me. Happy enough that I never thought to stop and ask Arthur how it was that the only city where we made any money was the one I controlled. To me, that was just more proof that I knew what I was doing and Arthur didn't. At least that's what I thought.

I wasn't all that concerned with how the tour, as a whole, turned out. After all, it wasn't as if I lost any of my money. For the guys in California, things didn't work out so well. They ended up losing all the money they invested in the show that, to Arthur, was just the cost of doing business. To me, he was being short sighted. In my mind, as long as everyone was making money, I would always be able to go back to them for more, like I had with David Brooks. Arthur didn't see things that way.

A few weeks after our initial conversation, Nia called and said she found this guy who had written a play and thought we should meet. He was putting it on at a church in Montgomery Alabama so we agreed that I'd fly in, meet him and check out his show. I'm fairly certain Nia had never seen or read his play before that night in Montgomery. I just think she knew I was looking for someone, and he was the first person she ran into who had what I needed. Beyond that, this was just a way for her to make a quick buck if I decided to do a deal with this guy.

To say I had low expectations is an understatement. I just kept telling myself I didn't have to like the play; I just had to be able to sell it. With that in mind, I got on a plane, flew into Birmingham and started the hour long drive to Montgomery. Little did I know those would be the last sane 60 minutes I would have for a very long time.

CHAPTER
5

Meeting the Man

The only reason I agreed to go to Alabama was because I had to at least make sure this was going to be something I could market. Other than that I had absolutely no expectation of liking or enjoying the show myself. To be honest, I had pretty much resigned myself to not liking whatever this was going to be. I was there solely to see if there was anything remotely sellable about this project and, if so, I had what I needed.

I had a friend in Alabama who lived about an hour away from the church where Nia told me the play was being performed. I asked him to pick me up at the airport and go with me to see the show, to which he replied something along the lines of "hell no" and a few other things I wouldn't repeat in polite company. I couldn't blame him because I would have probably responded the exact same way.

I kept working on him until I persuaded him to change his mind and tag along with me. I'm sure I had to make some promise of a six-pack or a shot or whatever the liquid currency of the day was back then to get him to reconsider. Whatever the price, it was worth it. One of the reasons I was able to talk him into going was because, realistically, I didn't see any way we would be staying beyond the first 30 minutes or so. It wouldn't take me much longer than that to see what I needed and having him with me gave me a built in excuse to leave early. And, since he would be my ride, I wouldn't have to rent a car so he'd be saving me a little money.

The trip started off smoothly enough. My flight was on time and he was waiting for me at the airport when I arrived. The ride to the church was fairly uneventful and since we hadn't seen each other in a long time it gave us a chance to catch up. As we got closer to our destination, I started looking around. That's when I became a little confused.

Looking out the window, I didn't get the impression we were driving into any kind of city. It felt like quite the opposite. When he slowed down and pulled up into the parking lot of the church, I became downright distraught. I thought back to that episode of Sanford and Son where Fred flew back to Saint Louis for an inheritance only to realize that his uncle didn't leave him any money. Upon being told there was no money coming and that he had gone all the way to Saint Louis for nothing, Fred replied with his typical, succinct eloquence, "I'll be damned!" Well, when we got to that church and I realized this was the venue, I knew exactly what old Fred G. Sanford was talking about. I had just come all the way to Alabama for this?! I'll be damned!

My buddy must have noticed the look on my face because he immediately started laughing and gave me a look as if to say, "Fool, what did you expect?"

OK, I know I didn't expect much but this was not at all what I had in mind. I don't know why but it hadn't dawned on me before arriving that this play was being produced at a local church. All of my experience with gospel plays came through the radio station so I had only seen or dealt with productions that had significant budgets and were being produced at major, professional venues. That church was a lot of things, most of them probably very good. What it was not however, was a professional theatrical venue.

To make matters even worse, the parking lot was damn near empty. There were, maybe, forty cars there and I figured some of those had to belong to the cast and crew. This was quickly turning from a nightmare into some kind of surreal Shakespearean tragedy. An empty parking lot meant an empty audience. An empty audience meant it would be way too noticeable for me to leave during the performance. So not only did I go all the way to Alabama to see this mess, but now I had to sit through the whole thing. I'll be damned!

We arrived a little bit late so, the few people that were there, were already inside. As we made our way across the unpaved parking lot, towards the front of the church I saw someone standing in the doorway. This had to be Nia. I called her when we were about 5 minutes out and she said she'd be waiting out front.

"Melvin?" she said as she came down the steps to greet us.

"Hey Nia," I replied as she extended her hand. "This is my friend Mark."

"Nice to meet you." She said, shaking his hand. "Y'all ready?"

"As ready as we're gonna be," was my reply as she turned and led us into the church. She took us through a side door that led down to the performance space and then through yet another door leading us back stage where the cast was waiting for the show to start. The show was cast with all local talent from the Atlanta area, so I had no idea who any of them were. As we went through the motions of meeting everyone, I slowly realized they were holding the show, waiting for me to get there. I would love to say this made me feel important but, to be honest, I started to feel kind of bad. In my mind, just based on the venue, the lack of name talent in the cast and the level of the production itself, I had all but decided this wasn't going to work for me.

The last person I met before taking my seat in the audience was the writer himself. He was also an actor in the show so he was backstage waiting with the rest of the cast. Nia led me over to where he was sitting and introduced us. "Melvin Childs, this is Tyler Perry, the writer and director."

If you ask me my first impression of Tyler back then, I would have to say the first thing that came to my mind was likable. From the time he stood up to shake my hand, I just found it hard not to like the guy. In the span of maybe 5 seconds, I went from looking out of the corner of my eye for the nearest escape, to sincerely rooting for him to do well, even without knowing anything about the man. He had a charm about him that seemed to come from a place of almost childlike innocence. It was both disarming and endearing and, in hindsight, should have been my first clue that he was a special talent.

He was also very timid, so much so that, as a man, I would call him soft. This was especially striking because of his size. Tyler stands every bit of six feet seven inches tall and probably weighed two hundred forty to two hundred fifty pounds back then. For comparison, I am only five feet six inches tall on my best day and yet I had the immediate impression that I could have taken his lunch money if I wanted to.

Our introductions done, it was time for us to take our seats in the audience. As I made my way to my seat, I noticed two things right away. First, there was hardly anybody there. I didn't count them but I could have if I wanted to. If I had to guess, I would say between thirty and fifty people in the audience. Second, the set consisted of some steps and a sheet with an apartment building painted on it. That was it. Now here I thought "Mama I'm Sorry" was a hot mess but at least they had a real set and Melba Moore. This show had a no-name cast and a damn sheet for a set. Tyler seemed like he was a nice guy and all but come on. A sheet?! Nia must have been out of her damn mind.

Now just about anyone who knows me knows that I have a very short attention span. It gets so bad that my friends are constantly telling me I have the attention span of a three year old. I don't care if it's a gospel play or the biggest Hollywood summer blockbuster, I have trouble sitting through just about anything over thirty minutes long. I say this because it was more than forty-five minutes into the performance before I even looked at my watch, and that was only because of the intermission!

Everything I had experienced before, in terms of a gospel play, felt like a sermon acted out on stage. This was different. It was more real. The dialogue felt authentic, like the way people I knew actually talked and the situations the characters found themselves in seemed like the kinds of things that happened in real life. The cast was very strong and even though the show opened with a song, as most of them did back then, the story was crafted in a way that kept the audience engaged and guessing what would happen next.

That was the other thing I noticed about the show. The audience reaction couldn't have been better if they had tried to stage it. The laughs came at all the right moments and, even with that small handful of people there, you could feel the energy in the room. It wasn't just that everyone was enjoying the performance. Like I said, all sixteen hundred and ninety-nine people at "Mamma I'm sorry" enjoyed that mess of a show. But this group seemed as if they were literally invested in what was happening on that stage. The characters and the story connected with this audience in a way that was special.

As for Tyler? Well, that timid guy I met backstage was nowhere to be found once the lights came on. He took the stage and, even amongst a very talented cast, stood out as something special. He had a charisma and a swagger on stage that you just can't teach. Most importantly, he maintained his like-ability. He connected with this audience in a personal way. He was one of them and they received him as one of their own. It was almost as if they shared some kind of special bond and I knew that if I could find a way to package this and get it out in front of an audience just like the one in Montgomery that night, there was no way we would fail.

Yep, I had found my show and could very easily have left then, knowing I had seen enough to be sold on the project. There was only one problem; I wanted to see the rest of the play.

6

I Don't Need You, I Got This

"Hey man, loved the show." I said, as I extended my hand to the star of the evening. "Seriously, it was really good."

"You need to go on somewhere with all that," was his response when he finally spoke.

"What? I just wanted to let you know I thought the show was good."

"Whatever dude. Ain't nobody tryin' to hear all that," he said as he put on his jacket. "Screw you."

OK, so it didn't exactly go like that. The point I'm making is that, as strange as it may sound, complementing an artist after a performance can be the absolute last thing they want to hear. I didn't know this at the time, but if the person has something financially invested in the show, which Tyler absolutely did, a pat on the back aint gonna cut it.

Just about every creative person who has ever done anything feels like what they've created is not only special, but also the greatest thing ever created. A serious artist has probably surveyed the landscape for things in his or her genre and found what they have done to be, not only comparable to anything else out there, but far superior. They simply don't understand why they're playing to empty houses in Alabama when "Mama I'm Sorry" is selling out two thousand seat theaters in Tulsa.

This is the mindset of most of the struggling artists I have come across and, a large part of me empathizes with them. When you put your heart and soul and, whatever little bit of money you have, on the line you do it with the belief that this is a calling. I have seen people sacrifice their jobs, their homes and even their families for the sake of their art. When I ask them why, they seem to always respond with some version of divine providence. They truly believe, in their very souls, that this is what they are meant to be doing.

So when someone like Tyler Perry puts on a show, for fifty people, in a small local church, in the middle of nowhere Alabama, he is doing so with the express purpose of being discovered. He figures all he has to do is put the show on and anyone who sees it will realize how amazingly talented he is. It's like that moment in the third act of a movie where the protagonist finally realizes what's at stake, the music reaches its peak, all of the conflict staged in the first two acts is suddenly, and miraculously, resolved and our hero has his "moment."

Well an artist like Tyler feels like every performance will be his moment. Every time he scrapes together enough pennies, makes a bunch of promises he can't possibly keep, and borrows money he has no way in hell of repaying, he does so believing that this time will be different. This time he will have his moment. Everything he's gone through has led him to this

very place and now it's his time. Once he can get that right
person to see what he's created, all doors will be open to him
and everyone will fall all over themselves with enough praise
and money to make everything worth it. He will finally have
been rewarded for his brilliance. This is the way a serious artist
typically feels and, in this way, Tyler Perry was no different.

The thing that made Tyler different was that, in his case,
he was right. He absolutely had something special, both in the
show he had written and created and in his own charisma on
stage. I made it a point to tell him as much when we met after
the performance.

I sat down with Tyler and Nia to discuss what I had in
mind for the show and, to his credit, he maintained a very even
temperament even as he was having his "moment." It had become
very clear to me that both Tyler and Nia viewed me as that
dude. You know, the guy with enough money to make things
happen. Someone in their position might sell a kidney to have
an audience with that dude; and here we were. I was telling them
how we were going to make this thing happen and I gave them
no reason to doubt I had the resources to do it. As such, they
treated me with deference, even though they knew next to
nothing about me.

I asked Tyler about the logistics of the production and what
it might take to put it out on the road. He assured me he had
everything worked out in his head, which impressed me because
I didn't expect for him to have thought anything like a
production tour through in any detail. I asked him to lay it
out for me and, as he began speaking, I realized that, in this
way, he was absolutely no different from any other artist I had
known—he had no clue what the hell he was talking about.

I'm sure he was well intentioned, but it was clear from the first few words out of his mouth that he didn't know the first thing about taking a show on the road. I laid out my plans for the tour, which amounted to a one week run in five cities. I told him we would be going to Tulsa and Oklahoma first, and then we would be stopping in Wichita and Little Rock before winding things up in Saint Louis. For those dates, he said he would need $25,000 total. Half of that would have to be paid to him up front and the rest at the end of the run. When he said the figure, I almost had to stop myself from laughing. There was no way in hell the show I had just seen was going to travel from Atlanta, Georgia to Oklahoma City and stay out on the road for a full week for only $25,000.

I asked him if he was sure of the amount and, again, he made it clear he had thought all of this through. He was convincing enough that I started to doubt myself. I figured maybe he knew something I didn't. At any rate, I was more than good with that number and would get back in touch with Nia once I had things set up on my end.

We wrapped up our meeting and I headed off to my buddy's house for the night. Nia and Tyler boarded the bus and, I guess, headed back to Atlanta. As happy as I'm sure they were, I was equally pleased with how the evening went. I came to Alabama hoping to see something half way decent that I could put up in Oklahoma and make a nice little pay day for myself. After seeing the show I left Alabama thinking I had something way bigger than that. I knew that if I could market it effectively, this would be something beyond anything I had in my wildest dreams. I was truly excited and couldn't wait to get back home and get started.

The first thing I did when I got home the next day was call David. I told him I had something to run by him and he told me to stop by the club that night so we could talk. It was a Sunday night so things wouldn't be too crazy, and he should be able to talk things through with me.

I got there at about eleven-thirty. There were people there but I wouldn't necessarily say it was packed. David was standing outside with the bouncers when I pulled up.

"Melvin Childs," he said with a big smile on his face. "What your ass need now?"

"Fool, I'm here to make you rich." I said without a hint of humor on my face or in my voice. I was dead serious.

"Well shit," he said with an even bigger smile. "Sounds like you and me got something to talk about. Step into my office."

With that, we walked over to a quiet area in the parking lot, and I broke down the whole story for him. I told him about my trip to Alabama and how good the show was. I told him about Tyler and how I thought he could be the next big thing, and how we would be able to get the show for next to nothing if we could move quickly.

"How much?" he asked, interrupting my stream of consciousness.

"Fifty."

"Fifty thousand?" he said skeptically "That don't sound like enough for what you talking about."

"Dude, he's gonna give me the show for twenty-five. The rest is enough to cover the venue deposits and the advertising, and you know I can do that shit." I could tell he was warming to the idea, so I kept going. "All you got to do is kick me down 50 g's, and we can go get paid."

"You know I ain't got no problem with getting paid Melvin Childs."

And with that, the deal was done. In truth, David was sold before I uttered a word. He had made so much money with me over the past few years that he had no reason to doubt anything I said. He was just surprised that I was asking for so little money.

Yes, I just said that fifty thousand dollars was a little bit of money. A promotion on the level I was talking about could easily cost twice that, but because of my position at the radio station and the other connects I had in the area, I knew I could do it for about half. Besides, Tyler was assuring me that he could get the show here for twenty-five thousand, only half of which, he needed up front. If things went smoothly, I might not even need the whole fifty!

I called Arthur after talking to David. I had everything in place at this point so I figured why not bring him into the mix. I told him the whole story, including how I had the money already lined up and how I had the cities and venues selected. I broke down how and why I selected the cities. Oklahoma City and Tulsa, for obvious reasons. Wichita and Little Rock because they were in close enough proximity to Tulsa to get the show there without too much trouble, and Saint Louis because it had a large enough black population to support multiple shows in a weekend. I told him what I had in mind for the marketing and how I would price the tickets. I had dotted every I and crossed every T before I ever called Arthur. There was no way he could poke any holes in my plan, and we both knew it. I was extremely proud of myself for putting this together and thought he would be to. I guess I was a little disappointed when I finished and all he had to say was, "Go ahead Melvin Childs. I hope you know what you're doing."

It stung a little bit but, if I'm honest, his condescending response shouldn't have come as much of a surprise. I loved Arthur, but he was always the type of guy whose interest in anything could be directly tied to what was in it for him. I honestly wanted to bring him on as a co-promoter or something, but when he responded the way he did, I guess I took it as disrespect. We were friends, true enough, but now it was time for me to assert myself in this relationship. The days of him talking to me crazy and telling me I didn't know shit were going to end at some point. Why not now? As far as I was concerned, it was WAY past the time for me to step out on my own and show him just how much I did know.

There is an old saying that respect is either given, earned or extracted. Arthur clearly wasn't about to give it willingly, so I guess I would have to go and get mine.

April 13, 1998

Mr. Tyler Perry
c/o ROSENSTONE/WENDER   *Ron Gu·azda*
3 East 48th Street
New York, NY 10017

Dear **Mr. Perry:**

Subject to due execution of this agreement by both of us, you (referred to herein from time to time as "Author") hereby grant to us an exclusive limited license to produce and present your Play entitled **I KNOW I'VE BEEN CHANGED** (hereinafter referred to as "The Play") in the English language in accordance with and subject to the terms and conditions herein set forth.

1. The Play shall be presented by us as a professional production at various venues in the United States during the period commencing **April 28 through May 17, 1999.** The rights granted herein shall automatically terminate if production does not open on or before date listed above.

It is also understood and agreed that if we do not present at least three (3) weeks of performances of the Play, within any six month period (beginning May 18, 1998), our rights in and to the Play shall terminate and revert back to the Author. It is further agreed that if we present the Play for a minimum of three (3) weeks within any six month period, our rights to produce the Play shall continue beyond May 18, 1999 at terms to be negotiated in good faith.

2. The Play shall be produced and presented by us only on the spoken stage with living actors in the immediate presence of the audience and in particular, the Play shall not be presented in whole or in part by film, radio, television or recording, including, without limitation, original cast recordings or phonograph records or tapes, or any other forms of recordings including but not limited to cassettes or audio-visual devices, now or hereafter devised. All rights in and to the Play not expressly granted to us hereunder are reserved to you and you may exercise same without restriction or limitation. It is understood that we

shall have the right to authorize one or more radio and/or television presentations of excerpts from the Play (each sum presentation not to exceed 5 minutes) for the sole purposes of exploiting and publicizing the production, and/or as part of critic's review.

       3. As consideration for this license we agree to pay you the following:

> **A non returnable advance of $20,000.00 payable: $10,000.00 on signing (receipt of which is acknowledged) and $10,000.00 on or before August 15, 1998, for any performances which may occur between May 18 - November 18, 1998.**
> **Against a royalty of 6% of the gross box office receipts**
> **With a minimum weekly guarantee of $5,000.00**

3(a) It is agreed that for a maximum of twenty four (24) performances only, which shall occur between April 28 - May 17, 1998, we agree to pay you, and you agree to accept from us, a royalty of three percent (3%) of the total gross box office receipts, with a minimum guarantee of $15,000.00

       4. All payments and all notices to you hereunder shall be made to and in the name of your agent, ROSENSTONE/WENDER, 3 East 48th Street, New York, NY 10017 attn. Ronald Gwiazda. It is understood that we shall supply to you, on a weekly basis, appropriate statements indicating the gross box office receipts signed by the treasurer and/or the exact number of performances given as may be applicable. It is understood that all payments of royalties will be made no later than seven (7) days following the end of each playing week.

       5. You shall receive billing credit, preceding the title, as the sole Author of the Play, whenever and wherever the title appears, as follows:

Tyler Perry's
I KNOW I'VE BEEN CHANGED

travel (where applicable) outlined in Exhibit A. It is understood that we are under no obligation to request your presence at promotions for the Play. If the terms outlined in said Exhibit A cannot be met, it is agreed that we must receive your written approval before making any such changes.

ACCEPTED AND AGREED TO:

Very truly yours,

_____
TYLER PERRY

_____
SOLSTICE GROUP
by: Nia Hill

_____
SOLSTICE GROUP
by: Melvin Childs

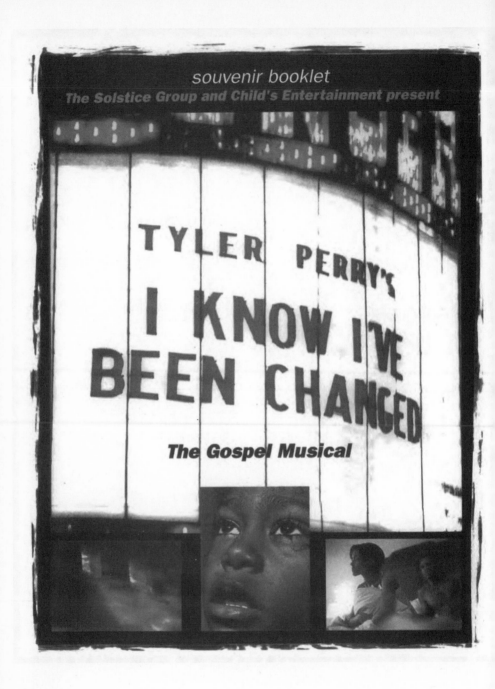

Who Are You Raising?

Why do you talk to your
child that way?
Don't you know them kids
believe what you say.

Don't tell him he's nothing,
nothing at all.
If that's what you tell him
don't be surprised when he fail.

Kids need to know they are
somebody too. What you
think about all this?
You better believe its true.

Who are you raising?
With all that yelling and
screaming you better
pray ask God to help you
 release that demon.

That child is the future
and you hold the key.
Be careful what you say,
be careful what you
let them see.
Who are you raising?
Letting that child
see all that crazy mess.
Who's fault will it be
when he's dead
before twenty~five,
take a guess?

Who are you raising?

Tyler Perry

Tyler Perry's
"I Know I've Been Changed"

From The Playwright's Pen...
To Parents

As I ride through the streets of the inner city, I see men with no vision, women with no hope and children with no future. It makes you ask the question, why? Why are our black men not living to see twenty-five? Why are our young women trading their bodies for crack cocaine? The answer is simple.

The life you live you become. The life you live before your children they become. Children mirror the image of their parents.

Love your children. Stand strong in your faith, teach your child to love now, teach them about God now, teach your child it is okay to walk away form a confrontation, teach your child that her body is a sacred temple. Teach them the power of prayer and show them the way to Christ, and when they are older, they won't depart from it.

Be careful what you say to your child, believe it or not, children remember everything you say to them and if you tell them they are nothing, that is what they will become. Without vision people perish. How can the child have a vision if the parents don't teach them to believe. Let's not create another generation of murderers and drug dealers!! Let's start giving God recognition, for He is the answer and should always be first in your life.

My advice to you is pray, seek Gods face, ask for all the fruit of the spirit, ask for wisdom to raise your children. Ask for peace to speak to them when you want to yell. Ask for Jesus Christ to protect your children and He will. Lay your hands on them while they sleep and just say "In the Name of Jesus!!" Plead the blood over them and I promise you He'll work it out.

Mother don't worry, Father don't cry... God is in Control!!

Tyler Perry's

"I Know I've Been Changed"

Tyler Perry's
"I Know I've Been Changed"

When someone reacts out of rage, the ramifications of that emotion and how they will impact others is not considered. Tyler Perry's "I Know I've Been Changed" illustrates the products of this unforeseen abuse and how it can leave eternal scars on the psyche of the recipient individuals.

The characters in this play demonstrate the different aspects of each of our own personalities and therefore touch audiences on a core level. Mary, the lead character, married and had two children before she had the opportunity to become an adult herself. Emotionally and spiritually irresponsible, she sought the succor of drugs to alleviate the pressure of rearing her children. This drug abuse manifests itself in verbal, emotional and physical abuse toward her children. She is unable to see the beauty of her own children, and addicted to drugs, unable to alter the destructive path she has embarked upon. Compounding an already dysfunctional family situation, the husband is abusive to his wife and children as well, molesting his older son which results in a dramatic plot twist later in the play.

Tyler Perry's "I Know I've Been Changed" demonstrates that children are definitely a product of their parents. "The life you live you become. The life you live before your children, they become. Children mirror the image of their parents." This gospel play motivates the understanding that although children are young, they absorb more than imagined, integrating their experiences into the adults they eventually become. It also recommends a spiritual discipline that teaches us to realize our words before they are uttered and consider the children we will inevitably impact. It teaches us to love.

Tyler Perry's "I Know I've Been Changed" is a remarkable piece as it addresses these complex societal issues while not losing sight of the value of humor. It transcends traditional play structure by elevating the audience to a new level of enlightenment, encouraging them to use the play like a mirror, and consider their own reflections.

Tyler Perry's
"I Know I've Been Changed"

Order of Show

Act One

Intermission

Act Two

Tyler Perry's
"I Know I've Been Changed"

The Cast

Shelia Stroud
AS MARY

Shelia Ranae Stroud is a native of Atlanta, Georgia. At the young age of twelve, she began singing and directing church choirs at her church; Hunter Hill First Missionary Baptist Church. She later began her formal studies at Clark Atlanta University, majoring in voice.

Since that time, Shelia has done just about everything. Roles in Off-Broadway Productions while recording and performing with the outstanding talent in Atlanta honed Shelia's raw talent. She has appeared by appointment as Guest Director for live recordings with Gospel-greats like Dottie Peoples and the People's Choice Chorale and Reverend Gerald Thompson and the Hy-Prayz Community Choir. Serving as choir coordinator for Jennifer Holliday's performance in the Harlem Nut Cracker (Jomandi Productions, 1994), and most recently, Diana Ross "Live at Chastain Park", (Atlanta, Georgia) expanded Shelia's scope of experience.

In 1994, she starred in "Dreamgirls"; "Sophisticated Ladies", the "Universal Big Top Circus", the 1995 Peach Drop "New Year's Eve Celebration" and was awarded "Best Female Vocalist" in 1991, and best supporting actress by the NAACP in 1997.

Lashun Pace
AS SISTER LEWIS

Lashun Pace was born into a musical family. She began singing with her sisters and the age of three and soon these women were known as the anointed Pace sisters. In 1988 Lashun pursued the solo career that god had ordained. Shortly thereafter, Lashun recorded In the house of the Lord" with Dr. Jonathan Greer and the Cathedral of Faith Choir.

Her vocal talents have been linked to other gospel greats such as : the Reverend James Moore, Karen Clark, an Edwin Hawkins, just to name a few. In 1990, Lashun received national acclaim when she recorded her first album entitled he lives, which yielded the signature song "I Know I've Been Changed" The album remained on the Billboard Gospel Chart for more than an year peaking at the number two spot.

Lashun's third album, "A Wealthy Place" is truly a musical masterpiece. It garnered her the 1997 Soul Train's "Lady of Soul Award" for Best Gospel Album of 1997. She has been the recipient of numerous gospel accolades including: The James Cleveland Excellence Award, The Bobby Jones Gospel Vision Award, and the 1991 Stella for best new artist. Her voice is the equation of her appointment and commission by God to deliver his message to the masses through song.

Tyler Perry
AS JOE

Tyler Perry is the writer and director of "I Know I've Been Changed" and brings his character to life like no other can. Mr. Perry studied under the creative genius of Ellis Marsalis at the New Orleans Creative School of the Arts. Tyler is an accomplished writer, who has just completed two screen plays that will soon be produced as feature films.

Recognized by contemporaries in his field, he recently worked with Lisa Wu-Sweat developing and directing her gospel play "A Change Gonna Come" featuring Todd Bridges and the Williams Brothers. His productions have received acclaim from institutions across the country as his plays tour extensively across the south and southeast.

Watch for his future productions Poppy's Seeds and Jazz Man's Blues as Tyler Perry takes his art form to another level.

Tyler Perry's

"I Know I've Been Changed"

The Cast

QUAN HOWELL

Quan Howell relocated to the Twin Cities of Minnesota to become a featured vocalist for the Grammy Award group, Sounds of Blackness. He appears on their "Time For Healing" album that debuted in 1997. He also co-wrote one of the singles entitled, "Crisis". His most recent projects are on the soundtracks for 'The Apostle' and the UK release of 'Hercules'. This native of Columbus, Ohio is no stranger to the stage, he has appeared in several productions including 'If Loving You Is Wrong' starring gospel great, Shirley Murdock. Quan's very dynamic vocals compares to such music great's as Luther Vandross, Stevie Wonder, Peabo Bryson, and Darryl Coley.

Ann Nesby
AS FANNIE

Ann Nesby began her vocal career as a young girl singing at Mount Zion Baptist Church in Illinois. She began sharing her innate vocal talent as the lead vocals of the Sound of Blackness. She was featured on such hits as "Optimistic", "I believe" "Testify", and "I Going all the Way". Her newly released album, "Here for You" developed by superstar producers Jimmy Jam and Terry Lewis, features hit singles "I'll Do Anything", "I'm Still Wearing Your Name".

Ann Nesby also writes and arranges her own work as well some material for gospel greats like Patti LaBelle and Gladys Knight. In 1991, She was awarded the Grammy Award for "Best Gospel album by a Choir", which led to another Grammy two years later for " Handel's Messiah - a soulful celebration".Her stunning live performance has been showcased at the Grammys, Essence Awards and the Soul Train Awards.

As the lead vocalist with the Grammy winning much acclaimed "Sounds of Blackness", Ann Nesby powerful vocal presence has legitimately earned her the often times overused tag of Diva. Her voice rich, commanding and passionate used as an instrument of truth. She is blessed with the ability to reach out and touch with her god given will.

JAMECIA BENNET

Jamecia Bennett possesses more vocal and stage experience than most of her peers. Having sung backup for the likes of Janet Jackson, Johnny Gill, Ann Nesby, Alexander O"Neal, and a member of the illustrious Sounds Of Blackness, Jamecia already has a resume to envy. Singing in the church at the age of three, it came as no surprise that Jamecia would have a bright future ahead of her. After extensive world touring with the Sounds Of Blackness, Jamecia decided to venture off on her own inking a recording contract with Mercury records which resulted with songs on the "Jason's Lyric" and "Kazaam" soundtracks. Jamecia is now featured vocalist, on the newly released "James Greer and Co. CD, "Don't Give Up" which is currently climbing the Billboard and gospel charts.
Jamecia has made appearances on the Bobby Jones Gospel show, performed concerts with Darryl Coley, and Sharon Clark-Sherard.
What's next for Jamecia you might ask? I'm ready to venture out on my own in pursuit of a new recording contract.

Tyler Perry's
"I Know I've Been Changed"

The Cast

**Carl Pertile
AS MITCH**

Carl Pertile was lead singer of the group Eboni, that was undefeated in Ed McMahon's Star Search and went on to become Grand Champions. A native of Midland, Texas, Carl has performed gospel, secular and classical music. He has performed with Grammy-award wining director Robert Shaw and the Sante Fe Opera. Carl's theatrical career began with Jomandi's MadHearts, where he was discovered by the road manager of the Sounds of Blackness. His vocal talents are heavily demonstrated on the Sounds of Blackness new album Time For Healing. He also displays his writing capabilities on the album with the song Crisis. He has recorded on several artists projects including, Rod Stewart, Jon Secada and Phil Collins.

A native Virginian, Bernadette Grant was blessed to be surrounded by music most of her life. Born to a family of singers, she discovered her love and aptitude for music at a very early age. However, it was only after arriving in Atlanta GA that her desire to explore the boundaries of her talent took root. In 1995, Tyler Perry's "I Know I've Been Changed" encouraged her acting wings to open up and take flight.

For her, music sooths the spirit and heals the soul. With that belief, she's performed for local charity events that support youth support services and musical education. Her quest to touch people's lives with her sultry voice, both in song and on stage, goes on.

**BERNADETTE
GRANT**

Sylvia Cannon is originally from the state of Mississippi. At the age of 15 she and her family moved to Atlanta. She began her professional career as a stand-up comedienne at the age of 19 yrs old. God has blessed her to appear on such television programs as HBO Def Comedy Jam, Apollo, BET's Comic View, BET"s Teen Summit, The Wayans' Brothers Show, the movie First Kid, And the talk show Vibe. She has also had the opportunity to perform with such gospel artists as Vanessa Bell Armstrong, Daryl Coley, and The Winans.

**SYLVIA
CANNON**

Additional Cast:

Lequita	Silivia Cannon
Sam	Darnell Harris
Ellen	Saycor Sengbloh

Tyler Perry's

"I Know I've Been Changed"

The Producers

Nia Hill
EXECUTIVE PRODUCER

Within the past decade, Ms. Hill has established herself as a producer in every right. She began her career in Jerez, Spain by producing and coordinating shows for the Jerezian government. In 1993 she relocated to Atlanta, and started an entrepreneurial path into the entertainment industry. She started her own company, "The Solstice Group," and began promoting a variety of independent concerts for artists like Natalie Cole, Patti LaBelle, Kirk Franklin & The Family, Jennifer Holliday and Jean Carne and gospel artists Yolanda Adams, Witness and John Pike. She also works with child star Raven-Symone (The Cosby Show and Hangin' with Mr. Cooper) and co-produced television commercial spots for the 1996 Atlanta Paralympic Games, in addition to the history making "Good News with Raven-Symone" for NBC's Atlanta affiliate WXIA Channel 11 Alive News.

In 1995, Ms. Hill used her substantial reservoir of knowledge to work with members of the state legislature to coordinate relief efforts to the victims of the tragic bombing in Oklahoma City, her hometown. She has continued to be a formidable force in the production arena, and is currently producing in the realm of feature films.

Melvin Childs
EXECUTIVE PRODUCER

Beginning his career in the late 1980s in radio after receiving his B.B.A. in Marketing, Mr. Childs saw his future unfold. Always thirsty for knowledge, he learned from the best and established a network of the most influential touring promoters in the nation. By 1992, he solely produced his first concert and has since worked in various capacities with the greatest performers in the United States today, including: Frankie Beverly and Maze, Boyz II Men, R. Kelly, Exscape, Queen Latifah, L.L. Cool J., Al Green, The Whispers, The Manhattans, The Chilites, Alex Buynon, Najee, Art Porter, Usher, Blackgirl, Total, Notorious B.I.G., and Craig Mack, to name just a few.

Mr. Childs' theater experience includes consulting for the musical stage play "Young Man, Older Woman" starring Millie Jackson and a partnership in the hit gospel play "He Say, She say, But what does God Say?" starring Kirk Franklin and the Family, Bernadette Stanis, Earnest Thomas, and Cheryl "Pepsi" Riley.

He has worked with record labels Arlista, Kaper/RCA, Laface, Bad Boy Entertainment and others. He believes that his greatest accomplishments have come form being truly blessed and working as well as learning from only the best in the business.

HAIR AND MAKE - UP	Juan Hughes
MUSIC DIRECTOR	Elvin Ross
PRODUCTION MANAGER	Juan Fontenout
ADDITIONAL PROMOTIONS BY	Black on Black Entertainment
COMPANY MANAGER	Belinda Reed

For Information or Questions
E-mail Address apotr @ aol.com

Tyler Perry's
"I Know I've Been Changed"

A Message To You

So why are you depressed?
You get that way at times.
Don't you know God loves you for who you are.
I know you are saying it's because of my mother
or because of my father that I am this way.
you are fighting the wrong battle.
Acknowledge what has happened to you
and give the whole situation to God
and He'll work it out.

God is the only answer to that situation.
Don't give it that much energy or thought.
Give it to God and He'll work it out.
JESUS is the answer.

Mr. Perry would like to thank

My heavenly father, who loves my soul so He gave me this ministry

The Solstice Group
Nia Hill,another show, another argument, and the love still grows.

Off the Chain, Chico Zavalla and Sonya Taylor

Lisa Watson and Jomandi Productions

Shelia, Chandra, Ann, Shun, Byron, Carl, and the rest of the cast thank you for letting
the vision be mine.

My M.D. Darius Green and the band and crew thanks for putting up with me

Lisa Sweat ~ I love you girl

Shirley Murdock thanks for listening then encouraging

Felicia Brown and Shenita Shorts ~ You love me and you pray, what else do I need?

Melvin Childs with Child's Entertainment

Preston Elliott and The Elliott Group

Thanks, I Love You Guys
Be Blessed.

One day I sat down to watch the evening news. I heard a story that sent chills up my spine. There was a man who wanted to commit suicide. He put a shot gun into his mouth and demanded that his four year old son pull the trigger, he did. Killing the man he called daddy. My first thought as I listened to this tragic story was, 'Who is this child and why is the devil trying to destroy him at such an early age?'. In the bible we read of stories, of kings ordering the deaths of male children, because one of them was special. These same orders prevail today. Kill and destroy our children. Just as the enemy has his orders, I have been given orders as well. I've been commissioned to help change a generation through an anointed gospel musical called 'I know I've Been Changed'. My orders are clear; show the people that being a parent is more than just being a provider. Its an appointment by God to oversee the structuring of a human life, to add positives to an ever-hungry but always negative world.

We must lead by example, rule with wisdom and pray with unwavering faith knowing that if we work with the knowledge of God, He will direct our paths.

The Solstice Group
presents

Tyler Perry's

"I Know I've Been Changed"

A Gospel Play

Please write to us and let us know
how this show has touched your life

The Solstice Group
745 Hansell Street SE
Suite 311
Atlanta, GA 30312

For Booking Information Contact
The Solstice Group (404) 622.4742

CHAPTER

7

This S**t Ain't Easy

I immediately got to work setting everything up for the tour. First, I called Tyler and told him the news. Then I called Nia and told her I needed her help. I still had my job at the station so I knew I wouldn't have time to do everything myself. Some of the leg work required to put this together would have to be done by someone other than me. Normally, this is the kind of thing I would have used Arthur for, but since I was hell-bent on showing him I could do this on my own, he wasn't an option. That being the case, I thought of Nia. She was someone I trusted and besides, I knew she would jump at the chance to solidify her place on the project.

Even though Nia was the one who introduced me to Tyler, there really was no obvious role for her to play on the team. Hence, there really was no way for her to get paid unless I found her a job on the project. She wasn't part of Tyler's creative or production teams, such as they were back then, and she had nothing financially invested in either the show or the tour. At most, I could have justified giving her a finder's fee, but that really was about it.

The fact that Arthur had talked himself out of the project is what opened up the door for Nia to come on board in an official capacity. To that point, we had never worked together on anything but had built a rapport through our contact at the radio station. I was honestly looking forward to working with her and thought to myself how nice it was going to be to do a promotion without Arthur's overbearing personality looming over everything, criticizing every decision. I was going to run this show and I was determined to do it my way.

Once Nia agreed to come on board as a producer, I sent her the contact information for the radio stations outside of Oklahoma City and Tulsa. Her first job was to start reaching out to them, getting them ready for the promotion. I never thought to ask what her background was or what kind of experience she had working with radio stations. As far as I was concerned, she used to call me at work several times a week so she had to know what she was doing. Not that it mattered all that much. I fully intended to oversee every last detail of this project and I would make sure everything was done right. This had the potential to be huge and I wasn't about to let it fail. I threw myself into the planning process so completely that everything else in my life became secondary. While this type of commitment is usually what you would look for in a successful entrepreneur, my situation was a little more complicated, still had a job.

Over the years my boss had become increasingly annoyed at my side projects. He felt I should be dedicating all of my time to selling ads for his stations instead of trying to make a name for myself as a promoter. At the very least, he expected my day job to take priority over anything else during business hours. I understood where he was coming from and, for the most part, I always managed to keep my personal projects from affecting my job responsibilities, but that wasn't the case this time around.

With this project, there was so much to do that something had to give. I wouldn't say I blatantly ignored my job, but I would also have to admit I wasn't very concerned with things like punctuality or keeping regular hours. I was late just about every day and, if something came up for the tour, I wouldn't hesitate to leave the office without telling anyone where I was going or when I'd be back. I was as driven to succeed as at any other time in my entire life, either before or since. I was also filled with the arrogance of youth and thought myself to be indispensable to the station. After all, I was the one with all the contacts and I was the one all of the promoters wanted to deal with. My boss could get frustrated all he wanted, but when it came right down to it, he needed me as much as I needed the job; maybe even more so, at least that's what I thought at the time.

It might have been more manageable if all I had to worry about were the typical responsibilities of a promoter. Unfortunately the more I talked to Tyler the more it became clear he had no idea what he was doing. We were in constant communication and it didn't take me long to figure out that if I wanted this thing to happen, I would have to help him . . . The problem was I didn't know a whole heck of a lot more than he did back then. I did know a thing or two about the logistics of putting a show on the road so I was able to help him with chartering a bus, finding accommodations and setting up a show schedule.

I didn't mind assisting and actually enjoyed working with him quite a bit. Tyler was a really humble, unassuming kind of guy back then, and we developed a real camaraderie as we learned the ropes together. We both felt like this was a huge opportunity, and he was as determined as myself to make the most of it. The only issue was the time it required for me to help him. Every minute I spent doing his job was another minute I spent not doing mine. As arrogant as I was, I still knew this couldn't go on forever. Eventually my boss would get fed up and have to do something. I just wanted to make it through to the end of the tour. I wasn't so much concerned with the paycheck as I was with the deeply discounted rate I was getting on advertising at both of his stations. That "special" rate the stations gave me was a key part of my plan and I couldn't afford to lose it. So I did my best to toe the line and maintain the status quo. The way I figured it, once this little mini tour was over, I would have enough money to take the show on the road in a real way. At that point my boss could do whatever he wanted because I wouldn't need the job anyway. I just had to get this show up and I would be set.

The other thing I realized from working so closely with Tyler was that there was no way in the world twenty-five thousand dollars was going to be enough for him to put the show up for a week. So at this point I had already given him his deposit, and met my pre-show financial obligation to him. Our deal was very straightforward, $25,000 for the show itself plus a standard three percent royalty for him as the writer. The royalty was to be paid to him weekly and since the run was only one week, I didn't have to give him another dime until after the last night of the tour.

That didn't stop him from asking me for the rest of the money three weeks before we opened, and it didn't stop me from giving it to him. In all honesty I had seen this coming so I had some time to think about what I would do once he asked me for the balance up front. I really didn't have any personal issue with helping him out. I figured we were in this together, and it was my job to have his back. The issue was business related.

I was already managing this project with no margin for error, and by giving him that extra $12,500, I would officially be underfunded. Meaning that if anything went wrong, anything at all, I would have no money in place to fix it. David had warned me that I wasn't asking for enough money so going back to him for more wasn't an option. There was no time to find another investor so, from a purely business perspective, it made absolutely no sense to give Tyler that money. In fact, it was the height of stupidity, which is why I did the obvious thing—I sent him a check within twelve hours of him asking for it.

About two weeks before opening night, I checked the sales numbers and was happy with where we were at in Tulsa and Oklahoma City. Wichita and Little Rock were a different story entirely. Sales were slow to the point where I was concerned. We had a decent promotion going in both markets but, for some reason, it just wasn't working. At least not fast enough. I couldn't count on any word of mouth in either city because we were only doing one show in each. Under normal circumstances, this is where you adjust, maybe you buy more ad time, tweak the promotion, increase the giveaways, print more flyers, etc., etc. Well all of those things cost money and guess what? I didn't have any.

I shut the book on Wichita and Little Rock. There wasn't anything I could do about it so I figured I might as well look at Saint Louis, in search of some better news. What happened next seemed to move in slow motion. I must have stared at the number for a good ten minutes before moving. I couldn't believe what I was seeing and yes, I said number. As in single digit and yes I just said single digit . . . as in zero.

They say adversity is the best teacher of all and I have found that to be true in my life. Unfortunately, up to that point, I had faced precious little adversity as a promoter so I honestly didn't know what to do. Two weeks before the show opened, and we had sold exactly ZERO tickets in our largest market! This wasn't happening. I took a look at the ad package Nia had purchased and the only thing I could think to say was, "I'll be damned." All of our spots, every single one of them, was running during over nights. Nia had actually bought the rookie package!

The rookie package is a block of advertising we would sell to first time promoters who didn't know any better. It consisted of a block of ads, all running in the middle of the night, that didn't have a chance in hell of selling a damn thing. We could sell them only to promoters who didn't know any better so we called them the rookie package. Not only that, but the rookie package rarely came along with any kind of promotion. It was a complete and utter waste of money, and I just found out it was one hundred percent of our advertising in our largest market.

It wasn't Nia's fault. She didn't know any better, which is why I was supposed to be monitoring the situation, making sure everything was done the way it needed to be. But between my day job and working with Tyler, I had simply spread myself too thin. It was obvious now that I had let some things slip. The sensible thing to do, under the circumstances, would have been to cancel the show. At a minimum, I should have cancelled everything outside of my home markets. If I had been thinking logically, I would have done exactly that and lived to fight another day. If only I had been thinking logically.

8

Help, I'm Drowning

At work, we used to laugh at the out of town, first time promoters who would call the station wanting to do projects. Nine times out of ten they didn't have a clue what they were doing, but because they were from some big city they always thought they knew more than we did. They were condescending to the point of being disrespectful and, in return, we would sell them some of the most worthless ad packages possible. Time after time, I saw these guys come through town and, literally, lose every dime they invested. I used to think it was funny. In fact, Arthur and I used to laugh about it all the time.

Every time I looked at the ad package we bought in Saint Louis, I thought of all those times I laughed at the expense of some poor fool from L.A. or New York. It never mattered to me that this was a person losing their hard earned money. I didn't think about whether they needed that money to pay their bills or feed their families. None of that was my problem. It wasn't my fault they didn't know what they were doing. All I knew was they had pissed me off and I took it upon myself to teach them a lesson.

My mother used to say that God don't like ugly. Some people might say what goes around comes around, or that you reap what you sow. However you want to phrase it, right now I was learning the first of many hard lessons, one of which was karma is a bitch.

It was one week before we opened and nothing much had changed. Tulsa and Oklahoma City were doing fairly well but not nearly good enough to make up for the coming losses in Wichita and Little Rock. And don't even get me started on Saint Louis. With no money and no time, I was out of options. I told myself all I had to do was get the show opened and things would turn around. I was sure that once an audience got to see it, they would fall in love with the product and we would be on our way. I just had to make it to opening night and we would be okay.

We opened to about nine hundred people on a Tuesday night in Tulsa. Tyler absolutely killed it. As much as everyone will point to Atlanta as the city that kicked him into the next level of stardom, the foundation he laid in Tulsa that night went a long way toward establishing his presence in the middle of the country. To his credit, even back then, Tyler insisted on addressing the audience after every performance. Nia and I were skeptical at first but it was clear that the audience loved this guy. Making his comments after the show just allowed him to solidify that bond. Looking back, it is clear what he was doing—he was establishing his brand.

Wednesday night in Oklahoma City went similarly well. Almost everything I thought about both him, and the show, was proving to be true. The audience reaction was off the charts and he left both cities with a fan base hungry for his return.

By any objective measure both promotions were a success. We came out of both cities with about eight thousand dollars combined and customers who were beyond satisfied. There was one small problem—I needed ten grand to guarantee the dates for the rest of the tour.

I was officially getting nervous. With the eight grand I had, I figured I could stretch that enough to make it through the week but if we did manage to make it through Saint Louis and things turned out badly, I wasn't a hundred percent sure I would have enough money to get home. That's how tight things were and, as it turns out; I wasn't the only one in financial trouble.

Tyler wasn't supposed to be paid any more money until the end of the week when he would get his royalty check. Well, that was fine in theory, but by the time he arrived in Tulsa for opening night, he was broke. I mean he was broke to the point of skipping meals and things like that. He was too proud to admit it, but I could tell by the way he acted whenever something came up where he might have to spend some money. We would ask him if he wanted to hang out with us and grab a bite to eat or something and he would always decline in a way that made me feel like he wanted to, but couldn't.

I figured out what was going on and started picking up the check for him whenever we went out. I didn't want him feeling left out, and I couldn't exactly have the star of the show sitting in a room starving now could I? Besides, having gotten to know him over the past six weeks, I rather enjoyed his company.

This probably won't come as a surprise to anyone reading this, but Tyler Perry is a funny guy. I had some of the best times of my life just kicking it with Tyler and Nia at a restaurant after a show. We would eat, drink and laugh until my face hurt. His drink of choice was a Long Island iced tea, even back then he was very image conscious. Every time the waiter would sit his drink in front of him, he would immediately pass it to my side of the table. Then, whenever he wanted to take a drink, he would look around the room to make sure no one was watching him, take a quick sip and put the glass back down beside me. Eventually Nia asked him what the hell he was doing and he said he didn't want his fans to see him take a drink.

"Fool don't nobody know who you are," I said laughing loudly.

"Well maybe if your breath wasn't stank you might be able to sell some tickets and get me some fans." He replied instantly. That was Tyler. As timid as he was when we first met, Tyler was a blast to have around once I got to know him. He was never one for a big crowd, which I found odd considering he was such an amazing performer, but since it was mostly just Tyler, Nia and myself, he was perfectly relaxed and would let his guard down.

Eventually he broke down and asked me for an advance on his royalty check so that he could make it through the week. We're not talking about very much money, probably less than three hundred dollars as I recall, but I was in bad shape myself. I was gonna need every dime I could get my hands on just to make it through the week. I ended up giving it to him, mostly because I didn't want him worried about money. I wanted him to be happy and focused on his performance. If I had any hope of pulling off a miracle, I was going to need Tyler Perry at his best.

On Wednesday, we played to about four hundred satisfied customers in Wichita. Tyler and the cast were absolutely doing their thing. They brought it every night and we got nothing but rave reviews from everyone in the audience. I heard nothing but positive comments after every show.

"Oh my God, what a great performance!" said one lady as she was leaving the lobby.

"That was SO good! I want to see it again," said another.

One especially nice old lady came up to me after the Wichita show and gave me a hug. She kept going on about how this show was going to change lives and how much she loved Tyler. I smiled and thanked her for coming but, inside, all I could think of was taking her outside and running her down with my car.

Yes, I had officially become a starving artist. Only I wasn't an artist. I was supposed to be that dude. The one every real struggling artist wanted to meet. I was supposed to be able to get things done and here I was, hoping against hope, logic and common sense for some kind of miracle. Now I was the one willing to beg, borrow, lie and steal just to keep the show going. I was the one deluding myself into thinking that if I could just get the show through this week, something amazing would happen. Somehow the right person or people would see it and all the doors would open. I was now officially waiting for my moment.

It wasn't just that I had a lot of money invested in the show. I also had people counting on me to make this happen. Nia and Tyler were out here on the road because of promises I made to them. David had given me fifty thousand dollars of his money because I told him there was no way we could lose.

These were people I considered my friends and I was letting them down.

Little Rock was a disaster. We played to one hundred fifty people. I really felt like the walls were closing in on me but I had to keep my game face on. I was up front with Nia about what was going on but I couldn't let Tyler know how bad things were. Above all else, I still very much believed in him and this show so I needed him to continue believing in me. Of course, he's not blind. He could see all those empty seats, but I tried to never let him see how it affected me. I wanted him to always think I had everything under control. I wanted him to see me as that dude.

Saint Louis made Little Rock seem like Live Aid. We sold less than a hundred tickets . . . to FOUR SHOWS. The tour was officially over and, by any objective measure; it was a complete financial flop. A failure of absolutely epic proportions . . . I had a great show, led by an amazing performer and yet I still lost almost everything. The audiences loved it every night and it didn't matter. What did I do wrong?

The answer was a lot. I went out underfunded and allowed myself to become emotionally attached to the success of the project. I should have overseen the ad buy in Saint Louis and I should have never given Tyler the full twenty-five thousand dollars up front. There were a million things I would have done differently but, here is the ultimate truth of the situation, none of it would have made a difference.

What I was going through were the growing pains of launching a new show. This is what happens when you want to introduce something new to an audience. People aren't going to line up and throw their money at a show just because you say it's different from "Mama I'm Sorry," especially when they had no problem with "Mama I'm Sorry." Overnight successes happened in movies. In real life, a new artist needs to find that dude. And that dude has to believe in that artist so much that he is willing to eat all the losses that come along with building the brand. For anyone to tell you they did it all by themselves, they are either blatantly dishonest or divorced from reality. It just doesn't happen that way.

I was certainly willing to take those bullets for Tyler. I believed in him that much. My problem was; I didn't have it like that financially. After the final Saint Louis performance, I wrote the venue a check for ten thousand dollars even though I only had about $4,000 left in my account. It's not as bad as it sounds. I still had about $8,000 of David's money left so as long as I could deposit that before the check hit my account, I would have at least been able to say I had met all of my obligations.

That night, as I was sitting in the hotel with Nia, talking about what my next move might be, I got a call from Tyler. I could tell by the sound of his voice that he was about to ask me for some money. I wasn't surprised because I knew he had been counting on the royalty money to settle up some of his obligations. I also knew that since sales for the last five shows were basically nonexistent, those royalties had to be a lot smaller than he had anticipated.

When he came into the room, he thanked me for everything I had done for him and said that he needed a favor.

"What you need Tyler?" I said, knowing what was coming next.

"I don't have the money to pay the cast," he said somberly. I could tell it was killing him to have to ask, but he had no choice. "If I can't pay these actors," he continued, "they'll never work with me again and we won't be able to put the show back up. You think you could loan me the money so that they can get paid?"

"How much?" I asked.

"$12,000."

I was silent for a long minute. I had seen this coming, but I had no idea how much he was going to need. I fully expected him to need a few hundred. Maybe two thousand at the most . . . but twelve thousand?! That was all I had. Let me rephrase; that was all the money I could get my hands on, and it wasn't exactly mine. $10,000 belonged to the venue in Saint Louis, who did me a favor by taking a check for the balance and letting me put on the show over the weekend. Whatever was left rightfully should have gone back to David.

The only way for me to give Tyler this money, was to knowingly let the venue check bounce and give him whatever was left of David's investment, screwing over one of my best friends in the process. Keep in mind I had absolutely no obligation whatsoever to pay the cast. That was entirely Tyler's responsibility. I didn't owe Tyler or anybody else from the show, a dime. Any sane person would have told him no, apologized for not being able to help him, and wished him luck. So, of course, I gave him the cash that night.

So here I was, sitting in a hotel in Saint Louis, flat ass broke with no clue what to do next. I barely had enough money left to get myself home the next morning. I did still have one thing to be thankful for though—I still had my job.

Yes, the same job I almost quit in the run up to this tour. The same job I pissed on and took for granted for months was now my silver lining. As long as I kept getting that steady check, I would be able to bounce back. It would take some time, sure, but I would eventually be able to pay David back, pay the venue and hold things together while I plotted my next move. Furthermore, through my contacts at the station, I would definitely be able to find another investor and get my show back up. That was as good a plan as I was going to come up with that night anyway.

The next morning, it was snowing as I left the hotel for the airport. It didn't seem all that bad to me but my mind was on a few other things besides the weather. When I arrived at the airport, I was told that my flight had been cancelled and that I wouldn't be able to get back to Oklahoma City until the next day.

I won't say I was too upset by that. After what I had just been through, spending an extra day away from home seemed like a reprieve. Plus, I had no idea what I was going to tell David so being able to delay that conversation by even twenty-four hours, felt like a blessing.

I made it home the next day at about 10:00 am and went straight to the office. I was already late but that was nothing new. What was new was my sudden appreciation for steady employment. I was motivated and eager to jump back into things when I arrived at the station. Nobody was around in the sales area so I stopped by my boss's office to say hello and let her know I was back and that's when I saw the termination letter sitting on her desk.

CHAPTER

9

The Fat Lady's Warming Up

There is an old saying that nothing sets you free quite like a good, old fashioned, ass whipping. Well as I stood there staring at that letter, tears welling up in my eyes, I felt like the freest black man in America. And for the first time in a long while, I wasn't thinking about the show or Tyler or anything to do with the entertainment business. For the first time in months, the only thing on my mind was my family.

I had been so caught up in making a name for myself that I had neglected the people who should have meant the most. I was a married man with a child and if it seems odd that I'm only mentioning them now well, that's the point. I am not proud of this but back then, my family took a back seat to my ambition. Of course I told myself this was all for them as much as me, but that was nothing more than a self-serving lie. The truth is I wanted to make a name for myself because it was what I wanted and the fact that they could benefit financially was just a convenient coincidence. Like so many other things in my life, I didn't fully appreciate what I had until I was about to lose it.

Standing there that day, I was lost. I felt like I had failed and because I failed, I was afraid my family would see me as less than the man I wanted to be. I take great pride in caring for my family and it literally broke my heart to think about the promise I made to my son when he was born. A promise to honor, protect and provide for him. A promise I could no longer keep.

You've probably figured out by now that I was an arrogant guy, even by twenty-something standards. We all have our crosses to bear so I don't hide from it. I had the world figured out, or so I thought, and I wasn't shy about letting anyone know it. A part of me realized I had this coming based on the way I had been acting, but none of that self-awareness was going to help me feed my son.

I went home after being officially told I was fired and, in typical fashion, I shut out the world. I didn't even tell my wife right away. I just sat around the house, depressed, trying to figure out what to do next.

After two or three days, I decided it was time to get off my ass and make something happen. I had been ducking David since I got back from Saint Louis and the venue was calling me to discuss the ten thousand dollar check that had bounced to the moon and back. Everything was a complete mess, but sitting in my pajamas watching Jerry Springer wasn't going to fix anything, so I got myself up and made a plan.

The first thing I had to do was tell my wife I lost my job. Then, I would call David and tell him the situation. Those were gonna be two rough conversations so I would get them out of the way first. After that, I made a mental note to get the videotape of the show over to Arthur. While we were out on the road, I had the presence of mind to videotape the performances and, I figured if he saw how good it was, he would be willing to help me get it back up.

Just as I had finished working out my plan, my wife came home. I had rehearsed what I was going to say in my head so I stepped to her as soon as she walked in the door. "Baby, we need to talk."

"Sounds serious." She said as she put down her purse.

"Well, it kind of is."

She looked at me for a long minute before busting out laughing. "Damn you Melvin!" she said as she playfully threw her coat at me, "How did you know?"

"Know what?" I replied, completely confused.

"Oh stop . . ." she said dismissively. "I just found out yesterday so somebody had to tell you."

"Baby, I have no idea what you're talking about."

"Oh so you just figured out I was pregnant all by yourself?"

*   *   *

Needless to say, my wife's revelation about our new bundle of joy was a bit of a shock. As much as I wanted to put it off after hearing she was pregnant, I stuck with the plan and told her what was going on. She was surprisingly calm about the whole situation and simply asked me what I planned to do. I told her I needed to find a way to get the show back up.

She had seen the performance in Oklahoma City, and we had the entire cast over to our house for dinner before opening night. Meeting them in that way and seeing them perform the way they did in the show made everything seem more real to her. She knew the show was good and she saw, first hand, the level of my involvement. She encouraged me not to give up and told me she would hold things down at home so that I could focus on the show.

As blown away as I was at her reaction, I also felt a little undeserving. I screwed things up because of my arrogance and now my family had to bail me out. To this day, the whole thing makes me cringe every time I think about it. It's one thing for me to sacrifice and suffer for the sake of my dream, but they shouldn't be asked to carry the weight of my choices. I promised myself, then and there, that I would make it up to them.

With the conversation with the wife finished, I made my way over to David's club. He was waiting outside for me when I pulled up and told him we needed to talk. We walked over to the same corner of the parking lot where he agreed to give me the money in the first place; only this time there was no banter. My heart was racing, making it difficult to stick to the script I had already worked out in my head.

"What's goin' on Melvin," he started off, "I've been trying to get a hold of you for a week."

"I know dawg," I replied quietly, "I was just trying to figure some things out."

"What's up with the show?" he asked, clearly irritated. I knew David very well by this point and I knew him to have a pretty bad temper so I had to tread carefully with what came next.

"OK, here's the deal," I started off, "we got our asses kicked."

"How bad?" he asked. I wasn't ready to deal with that particular question just yet so I went ahead with my prepared statement.

"Look, obviously I should have called you when we got back; and, if I had anything good to say you know I would have."

"How bad?" he interrupted impatiently. I was out of time. He wasn't just going to sit there and let me try to soften the blow for the next twenty minutes. I instinctively took a step backwards before answering his question.

"Everything."

"Everything?" he asked incredulously.

"Melvin, how in the hell did you lose ALL the damn money?!"

He was right to be suspicious. I know he didn't think I would steal from him but it was unheard of to lose all of your money on any project. There should always be a little something left, even after the worst ass kicking in the world.

The problem is, there was no way in hell I could tell him I gave Tyler the rest of his money. Had I done that, I don't think I would have made it home that night.

"You were right," I continued "I was WAY underfunded and by the time I realized it, it was too late to do anything about it."

"So you lost all the damn money?

"Unfortunately yes. And I lost my job too . . ."

"What? How the hell you do that?" he asked as I successfully shifted the conversation away from the story of just how bad I had screwed up to just how badly I was getting screwed at the moment.

"It's a long story; but look, I swear I'm gonna make this right. You just gonna have to bear with me for a minute."

"Alright Melvin," he said suspiciously. "Let me know what's going on." And with that, he walked off, leaving me standing in the parking lot all by myself.

The next morning I dropped the video tape at Arthur's house. He wasn't home at the time so I left it with his wife and asked her to tell him to call me after he watched it. There wasn't much else for me to do at the moment so I just went home and started looking through the want ads.

This was mainly for show as I had no intention of going back to work at a regular 9–5 type job. I knew I needed to focus on getting this show back together and the only realistic way of doing that was to persuade Arthur to help me. He didn't bother coming to either of the shows we did in Oklahoma City or Tulsa, but watching the video should go a long way toward convincing him that I had something special on my hands. I just had to wait.

So that's what I did. A day went by. Then two. A week went by and still not a word from Arthur. I did, however, hear from Tyler.

"Hey Melvin, it's Tyler."

"What's up dude?"

"Look man, I hate to ask, but I don't have a place to stay right now. You think you could help me out finding a place?"

Tyler knew by now that I wasn't exactly rich, but he also had no idea I was as broke as I was. For my part, I always assumed he was having some major money issues, but I never thought he was going to be homeless. After getting to know him over the course of those few months, I considered Tyler to be a friend so when he told me he needed a place to stay I reacted, as you would expect a friend to react. I wanted to help. Unfortunately, as much as I would have loved to just reach in my pocket and give him some money, I was running on empty myself. So I did the only thing I could. I borrowed the money from my wife.

We set him up in a two hundred dollar per week hotel. OK so it wasn't the four seasons, but at least he wasn't homeless. My wife was OK paying for him at first but, over the course of the next few weeks, he reached out to me for money on several more occasions. It wasn't all the money in the world mind you. More like a hundred dollars here or a hundred fifty there so that he could buy food or essentials or whatever. The point is I never once turned him down. Of course I still had no income so all of this money was coming from my wife's paycheck—the only paycheck in our household.

She quickly grew tired of that situation. It was one thing to take care of her husband and her kids. It was another thing entirely to take care of some grown ass man living in Atlanta. A man she met exactly one time. That was asking a little much.

Needless to say things at home were getting really tense. I tried to convince her this was all an investment and that it would pay off one day when we got the show back up, but she wasn't trying to hear any of that. Eventually, as I'm sure you can imagine, her point of view became very clear.

"I don't want to hear about no damn play no damn more! You need to stop PLAYING and get a damn job."

I can't blame her. Any sane person would have reacted the same way. I was taking money out of our home, where we had three mouths to feed and a fourth on the way, and sending it to some guy living in Atlanta because he had written a play that

I liked. Of course I saw it as more than that, but if the shoe had been on the other foot, I can't say I would have been so willing to take food out of my kids' mouths to finance someone else's vision.

And therein lied the problem. I didn't really have a vision. Here I was asking my wife to support our family plus help Tyler; only I had no idea where any of this was leading. None of my so-called contacts I made while working at the station would take or return my calls now that I no longer worked there. And, I still hadn't heard from Arthur. I literally had nothing going on.

The situation at home had gotten to the point where I knew things couldn't go on the way they were. Only I had zero idea how to change any of it. I was stuck and it started to feel like the walls were closing in on me again, and that's when he called.

"Melvin Childs, you got a minute? I want to talk to you about something."

"Yeah I'm cool," I responded, trying to play it cool. "What you need Arthur?"

"Can you come by the house?"

"On my way."

I think I must've jumped five feet in the air. My mind raced through every tired cliché I had ever heard or read on a fortune cookie:

"I knew that if I stuck with it, something would break my way."

"The lord didn't bring me all this way to abandon me."

"All I had to do was persevere . . ."

The list went on and on. The point was I had been given a ray of hope and I wanted to run, as fast as I could, into the light.

I grabbed my stuff and made a beeline to Arthur's house. I couldn't wait to hear what he thought of the show.

Well, I would love to tell you what we talked about when I got to his house. The problem is, I honestly don't remember. He was going on about something he was working on, but all I could think was why isn't he talking about my show? This went on long enough to where I realized he had no intention of even mentioning the videotape or the show. The brief burst of excitement I felt when he called a few hours ago was now gone, replaced by the agonizing realization that there would be no miracle. I couldn't keep denying it any more . . . I lost.

As we were finishing up whatever we were talking about and I was getting ready to leave, I swallowed the last little bit of pride I had left and brought the subject up myself.

"Arthur," I said putting on my jacket "did you even watch the tape of the show?"

"Yeah Melvin," he said, rolling his eyes "I watched that bullshit. I told you, you didn't know what you was talking about. That shit sucked and you gonna keep getting your ass kicked with that mess."

That was it. I was in my car, driving home, planning what I was going to tell Tyler. Nia and I were in touch almost every day so she knew where things stood but Tyler was still under the impression that I was going to be able to get things moving again. I was going to have to tell him it wasn't going to happen. Arthur was my last shot.

I was sure that if he saw the show and, more importantly, Tyler perform, that he would see what I saw, but I was wrong. He wanted nothing to do with any of it and without his help, there were no more moves for me to make. I couldn't keep taking from my wife for something that I had no way of doing. I was going to have to start doing right by her sooner than later and the first thing I had to do was put an end to this fantasy.

The phone was ringing when I got home. It was Nia, which was good because I felt like she should hear the bad news first.

"What's up Melvin?"

"Well . . . I just spoke to Arthur . . ."

"Hold up," she interrupted, "before you get into that, I met this guy last night that said he wants to invest his money in a show."

CHAPTER

10

Hold the Curtain

*Again I tell you, it is easier for a camel to go
through the eye of a needle than for a rich man to
enter the kingdom of God.*

—Matthew 19:24

I realize I probably raised a few eyebrows earlier when
I suggested that hard work and faith were not the keys to
making it in the entertainment industry. I'm sure, to many of
Tyler's fans, that sentiment borders on blasphemy.

Well I have to stand by those words, and not because
I question the virtues of hard work and faith. I have to stand
by them because I know that the fruits of success in the
entertainment business are not of God and anything not of
God cannot be obtained through His grace. The excesses and
ego gratification that come as part and parcel to celebrity are
things of the world and in order to achieve worldly reward you
have to submit yourself to things that, by definition, fall short
of the glory of God.

This is not meant as an indictment of Tyler's character as much as it is a statement of fact. You do not achieve what Tyler, or any other celebrity, has achieved without being incredibly committed. People tend to toss around phrases like "meant to be" or "born to do this" lightly, treating them as meaningless anecdotes to mask the mundaneness of our daily lives. For someone like Tyler, these are not tired clichés. They aren't clichés at all. They are honest depictions of what lives inside.

To ascend to that level of celebrity, you have to want it to the point of desperation. It has to consume and dominate your every waking moment. It has to be the first thing you think of in the morning and the last thing you think about at night. And if you want something, anything, that badly you will be willing to do just about anything to get it. Show me someone as famous as Tyler Perry and I will show you someone who, at some point, sacrificed his or her integrity at the altar of fame.

What does any of this mean? Well I can state to you, unequivocally, that NONE of us; not myself, not Nia and not Tyler Perry had any illusions whatsoever about how Chico made his money. None. We didn't care—we couldn't afford to. All of us desperately wanted to get this show back up, and we were willing to do whatever it took to make that happen. Taking money from a drug dealer was never questioned. We saw it as a blessing because to us, he was that dude.

Now if you were to look up "that dude" in the dictionary you would probably find a picture of Chico. He had it all— designer suits, five hundred dollar shoes, expensive cars and a stable of beautiful women at his disposal. Everything about the man absolutely reeked of money.

Nia met him through a woman named Sonya Taylor. Apparently they worked together on a Lil' Kim concert Chico funded and Nia reached out to her to see if he might be interested in working something out with us. According to Nia, Chico was instantly interested and started asking a bunch of questions, which is when she referred him to me.

The first thing I thought when she was telling me this was, "fool, can't you see dude's just trying to get into your pants?" That might sound unnecessarily cynical, but keep in mind I didn't know Sonya or Chico. I just had my dreams destroyed by Arthur, my marriage was falling apart, I had no job, no money and a kid on the way. I didn't have the time or the patience to listen to some silly story about a knucklehead spitting some weak ass game at a naïve friend in Atlanta. I had grownup problems to deal with.

When she suggested I talk to him over the phone, I agreed. Mainly because I wanted to get off the phone before my wife came home. I never got to tell Nia how much Arthur hated the show, and I didn't want to have that conversation with my wife looking over my shoulder. Besides, it couldn't hurt to talk to the guy. If any of what he said was even half true, he might have some money to invest in something smaller. I didn't think there was any way he would have enough money to mount the show.

When I spoke to him the next day, he didn't do much to alleviate my concerns. I broke down the project and he sounded like he was interested. I asked him what kind of money he was looking to invest and all he said was, "Whatever you need."

I asked him what kind of terms he was looking for, and he told me we could worry about that stuff later. It was clear to me that he was completely disinterested in any of the financial details.

Nia and this Chico clown were wasting my damn time, and it was pissing me off. The whole thing sounded like complete bullshit. Anybody interested in investing money would absolutely have a dollar figure in mind if not a specific figure, then at least a range or maybe a maximum amount. This Chico character had none of that, and he didn't seem all that concerned with how he was going to make money. I made a mental note to cuss Nia out as soon as I had the chance.

He said he loved the idea and wanted me to come to Atlanta to discuss everything in person. This surprised me. If he was running some kind of game at Nia, the last thing he would need is for me to be in his mix. In that instant, I went from wanting to strangle her to thinking this guy might be worth checking out. If it sounds like I was all over the place emotionally, I was. That's the way this business works. You can be up one day and down the next. The key is to stay in the game long enough to bounce back after your losses.

Arthur had taught me that and he was right. Unfortunately in my case, I was out of money and time so there was no way I would be able to stay in the game so to speak. I had all but resigned myself to folding up shop and moving on to something else when Nia called so I, literally, had nothing to lose at that point. So even though I was still pretty sure Chico was full of shit, I had to check it out to be sure. There was one small thing I had to do before I took off for Atlanta.

"How much money we have in the house account?" I asked as my wife walked in the door from work.

"Why?"

"I need to go to Atlanta."

"What's in Atlanta?" She asked, almost casually, as she took off her coat. I knew what came next was going to set her off so I braced myself for the explosion.

"I think we might have found an investor to remount the show. I have to fly down and meet with him." I tried to sound excited, like this was a big opportunity for both of us, but I could see it wasn't working. She actually never responded and went about her business as if I had never asked her anything. At first I thought she was too pissed off to speak, but then I saw the look in her eyes. She wasn't pissed, she was hurt.

"I'll only be gone one day." I said, trying to get her to open up. I wanted her to yell at me, call me names, cuss me out, throw something at me, whatever. Anger I can deal with. But this was something different. I was deeply hurting someone I loved and there was nothing I could do to make it better. "I'll get the first flight back in the morning, I promise."

"Whatever, Melvin," was all she said as she left the room.

Chico set us up to have dinner at one of the best restaurants in the city. We arrived first and when we told the hostess whom we were meeting, we were immediately taken to the table. I have to say, I was starting to become increasingly curious about this Chico character.

"Nia, what is the deal with this guy?" I asked, still looking around, in awe of the impeccably beautiful dining room. "Does he really have it going on like this?"

Before she could answer, Chico and Sonya arrived. When he walked in the room, I knew he was for real. From my time at the radio station, I had been around enough people with real money to recognize the look. Chico had the look times ten but he carried it naturally. He didn't hide the fact that he was rolling but he never came across like he was flaunting it either. He just seemed to wear his wealth naturally, and it fit him like a glove.

I went over everything again. This time for both Chico and Sonya, a drop dead gorgeous black woman who was also supposed to be the CEO of his entertainment company. Half way through my spiel I noticed Chico wasn't listening and that's when it hit me—we were there as much to impress his girl as to sell the project. Looking back, I think selling/ impressing Sonya, the girlfriend/CEO, was the ticket to selling the project.

I immediately started directing all of my attention towards her. I poured on the charm extra thick and made it clear that I was pitching her as much as him. By the end of my proposal, I won't say she was eating out of my hands, but she was 100 percent on board with the project. The only things left to discuss were; how much money, how he planned to get it to me, and when he planned to do it.

We finished our dinner without discussing the project, and I actually enjoyed myself for the first time in months. We laughed and joked around until they were clearing the furniture from the tables around us, the universal way for the staff to tell you it's time to get the hell out.

"How much you need?" Chico asked as we gathered our things to go home.

"$100,000 would do real nicely." I replied.

"We split what comes back 50/50?"

"Right down the middle." I said confidently.

"Alright my man, come down to Miami and I'll take care of you." He said with a smile "Just let me know when you're coming."

After we said our goodbyes and they left, Nia and I sat down in her car to discuss what our next move should be. If he came through with the money, we would be able to put the show back up, and we agreed that Atlanta was the best place to do it. All of the talent was already there, the city had a large black community and there were some really nice venues to choose from. We talked for a long while about everything we needed to do and how we would do it. The more we talked over everything, the more excited I allowed myself to become. If Chico was for real, which I was fairly sure he was, I had just been given a new lease on life. Two days ago I had given up and was willing to accept my fate. Now? I was sitting in my friend's car plotting our come back. And as we sat there, I could feel my spirit being reawakened with each passing moment.

Hope is a very powerful drug. Without it, the human spirit just doesn't function properly. Before that dinner with Chico and Sonya, I felt deflated like my body was a beat up, 4-cylinder car, chugging along from point to point desperately in need of a tune up. After getting the thumbs up from the two of them, I felt like I was injected with some sort of super fuel. I instantly sprang to life and felt like my body was a brand new, 8-cylinder Porsche operating at maximum efficiency.

Both of us could feel the excitement growing. It was as if we had been given a stay of execution and we weren't about to let this opportunity go to waste. I can't speak for her, but I was literally intoxicated by the thought of being back in the game. I felt like myself for the first time since we wrapped up in Saint Louis and

I was determined to come back with a vengeance. I wasn't going to let anyone or anything stand in my way. I wanted this that badly.

We called and told Tyler what was going on and that he should just sit tight for a day or so while we tried to work out the details. I knew he was still staying in the hotel so I thought it was the right thing to do to throw a little hope his way as well. Needless to say he was excited and wanted to know when we had a plan in place to get back to work. We told him we would know something definitive shortly and that we would let him know the minute we did.

One of the other things we decided was that I would come back to Atlanta and stay there until the show was back up. Without saying it, we both knew this was our last shot at making something happen with this show, so everything else would have to take a back seat. Unfortunately for me, that included my family.

CHAPTER

11

Where Did YOU Think the Money Came From?

"Just act normal."

I hated Chico. His punk ass knew damn well I had never done anything like this before. He could've had one of his people bring me the money. Now I was about to go to jail while he was back in his mansion drinking orange juice with his naked chick. This was some bullshit!

"Sir, step forward please."

The voice of the security agent snapped me back to reality. I handed her my ticket and placed my new duffel bag on the conveyor belt. Since it was the only piece of luggage I had, I couldn't exactly prolong the process. The only thing in the bag was the money and I was hoping that wouldn't show up on the x-ray machine. Either way, it was too late to turn back now so I bit the bullet and stepped forward to the scanner.

The security agent sitting on the other side of the conveyor belt was a young black guy. He and I locked eyes as I stepped through. I had nothing on me to set off the body scanner so I was all good there. Now all I had to do was collect my bag and be on my way. As I stepped to the side to do just that, I noticed my young black brother intensely studying his x-ray screen. Oh shit . . .

I thought about taking off and running but there really was nowhere to go. I couldn't exactly plead ignorance as it was my only piece of luggage and everyone at the security station saw me carry it in and place it on the belt. I was stuck. He stopped the belt and got up out of his seat without looking over at me. Another bad sign was when he pulled the bag to the side and opened it up. "Whoa," he exclaimed as his eyes popped wide open. He stared at the contents for what seemed like an hour, but in actuality was probably only a few seconds. Whatever, it was long enough for him to realize what was in there. I was done and I knew it . . . damn. He looked up at me, paused for a beat, and gave me a subtle but knowing smile. He immediately zipped the bag, handed it to me, and said, "Go ahead man."

I know what you're thinking. No, my name is not Luke and I did not play some kind of Jedi mind trick on that guy. I honestly don't know what he was thinking or why he let me go. Maybe he felt sorry for me, seeing as I had to have the most pitiful, please-don't-send-me-to-jail look on my face when he looked up from the bag. Maybe he didn't want to do the extra paper work that would have come if he had me arrested, or maybe he just didn't want to send anybody to jail on that particular afternoon. Whatever the reason, I made it through. Now there was nothing standing in my way.

Nia was waiting for me at the airport in Atlanta. Since she had dropped me off at the airport that morning, she knew it was all good when she saw me with the new duffel bag. The first thing we did was call Tyler and tell him we were ready to get moving. We knew he was struggling so we put $1,000 in his pocket to keep him cool until we put everything together. We decided before I left that, if everything worked out, I would stay at Nia's place and we would dedicate all of our time to this project. Because that was now a reality, I had one more phone call to make before we could get to work.

"Hello."

"Hey baby, it's me." I said gently, trying to gauge her mood.

"When you coming home?" she said without a hint of emotion. She had been through a lot with me and I could tell she was just tired of all the drama.

"Well, we got the money for the show." I said, hoping she would at least be able to see how great it was, for both of us, that we had another chance.

"Melvin I told you I don't want to hear no more about no damn play! Now you told me you would only be gone one day. So when you coming home?!"

It wasn't so much anger as it was frustration. The woman was tired and probably felt like she was fighting to take care of our family alone. I'm sure if you were to ask her, she would say she felt abandoned. What I had to say next would not help her feel any better.

"Well, I'm gonna stay down here and work on this until we get the show back up."

"Whatever Melvin, I don't care what you do," she said without hesitation. "I have a job and I'll be here taking care of your family when you're ready to grow the hell up." And with that, she hung up the phone.

I wasn't surprised by her reaction; I could have predicted it. And I understood how she felt, but none of that mattered. I knew what I needed to do and where I needed to be to do it. This was my last chance and I couldn't afford for things to slip by me like they did in Saint Louis. Also keep in mind that the Internet was still relatively new back then and not everybody had a cell phone. If this had taken place today, it would be entirely possible to manage the situation in Atlanta from another city. That wasn't the case in 1998. If I wanted to make sure things went right, I had to be there.

Maybe I'm justifying a little bit, I can admit that. It was NOT an easy decision by any means to leave my family behind while I chased this dream. I was sick about it then, and I don't feel much better about it today, but I never once considered not doing it. This was my shot and I was going to take it, period. I wasn't about to let anything or anyone take this opportunity away from me.

Was it the right decision? In hindsight I'm not so sure. Like I said earlier, if you want something bad enough, you will be willing to do just about anything to get it. I am no different from anyone else in that regard. I walked away from a family that needed me and, essentially, left them to fend for themselves while I was hustling down in Atlanta, trying to launch Tyler Perry's career. Getting that show back up was my only concern. Everything else, including my family, was a distant second and would have to wait.

As ugly as that sounds, I was more than willing to make that sacrifice. You have to understand, it's not just the Will Smith's or Tyler Perry's of the world that make difficult choices for the sake of their dreams. Behind every Tyler Perry there is somebody else who is just as willing, if not more so, to do whatever it takes. Someone crazy or foolish enough to put himself in harm's way for the sake of something he or she perceives to be bigger than they are. Only their stories are rarely told because what they had to do is often contrary to the image that has been created for the celebrity in question.

But that doesn't lessen our contribution to their success. I have no problem recognizing Tyler Perry's talent but here is the worst kept secret in the world. You do not make it in this business based on talent. Talent is not enough. It wasn't enough then, it's not enough now and it won't be enough tomorrow. Without someone standing in the shadows, hustling and grinding for him, Tyler Perry is not Tyler Perry. He is just another cautionary tale of big, unrealistic dreams that come crashing down to earth at the feet of the monster we call maturity.

If Nia hadn't met Chico, I was ready to throw in the towel on this whole project and focus on my family. Tyler himself admits he was close to giving up before we did the House of Blues run. No matter how talented or passionate you are, no one chases a dream forever. There are tons of talented people who, without the support of someone like me, decide they can't do it anymore. They get tired of chasing something that seems, with each passing day, to be increasingly unattainable. Only, from the outside, you don't call it giving up, you call it growing up. And every struggling artist out there knows exactly what I'm talking about. They've all heard the speeches from their loved ones.

"When are you gonna get a real job?"

"What makes you think you don't have to go to work like everybody else?"

"You need to grow up."

What they don't tell you is that by growing up, they are saying you should accept your rightful place in a society of mediocrity. For an artist, any artist, this is a form of death. They have to sacrifice the creative voice inside of them in order to make a living and provide for a family. They are sentenced to silence, never to be heard from again. This is what happens to talented people who try to do it on their own. This is what happens if a Tyler Perry doesn't have help.

I can imagine what you're thinking and no, this is not about credit or financial gain. The money comes and goes as part of the normal course of doing business. I've said this before and I will say it until I'm blue in the face, Tyler Perry does not owe me a dime and, FYI, I have NEVER asked him for one. This is bigger than that. This is about honoring the bond we forge as brothers when we are all fighting for the same thing. This is about recognizing the sacrifices of others. Sacrifices made on your behalf to aid in your quest for success.

For anyone who doubts me, ask yourself this: "How does a homeless man go from sleeping in his car to performing at, and selling out, the House of Blues?"

He doesn't. It couldn't possibly happen. The story is little more than an absurd fantasy. I can't tell you how a homeless man could do anything close to that because it's simply not possible. Now if you want to know how Tyler Perry ended up performing at, and selling out the House of Blues . . . well that I can tell you.

CHAPTER

12

Fantasy Island

What's the first rule of promotions? Have something to promote. It's not exactly rocket science, but it's something that is completely lost on most creative/artist types. It doesn't matter how good your show is. If you want to make a living doing this, the only thing that matters is how you can sell it and who can you sell it to. The general public is typically very slow to accept something new, especially if, by acceptance, you mean they have to spend their hard earned money. This is as true for Tyler Perry as it is for Joe Smith playwright from nowhere Minnesota. People support what they know and if they don't know you, they are, at best, skeptical. At worst they can be downright hostile. This is the mountain a new artist has to climb, and how do they do it?

You start by earning some legitimacy and a large part of that is choosing the right venues. Certain venues carry with them a certain prestige and, with that, the assumption of quality. If you can tie your product to one of those venues, you'll have gone a long way toward starting your climb smoothly. You are, by no means, at the top, but you are at least off to a good start. And, you'll be exactly where Tyler was in 1998.

Nia and I immediately started calling around looking for venues to host the show. The Fox Theater and The Civic Center were the two largest and most prestigious in the city back then but they were also notoriously difficult to get into. For a place like the Fox, it wasn't unusual for acts to book a year in advance, and we were looking to do something in 8 weeks.

When I called, the manager basically laughed at me, asked who I was and told me there was no way they could help us. I got the distinct impression he didn't think I knew what the hell I was doing. The response from The Civic Center was not any better. We called every venue we could think of and nothing was available on such short notice. We were stuck.

Nia had done some work at a place called the Tabernacle. It was an old church near Olympic Village that had been converted into a performance venue. The intriguing thing to me was, during the Olympics, the building was converted into a House of Blues club. There was still a lot of residual buzz about the '96 Olympics in and around the city so I figured if we could find a way to leverage some of that hype, we would be good to go. The key was to keep calling it the House of Blues even though it was technically not anymore. We needed that name to give us the legitimacy we lacked with a new show and an unknown writer.

Nia knew the general manager so she made the booking. Looking back, it really was the perfect place to host the show, but I would be lying if I said the choice was intentional. It was a venue designed primarily for musical acts, which is why we didn't look there in the first place. There were regular theater style seats upstairs, but down on the main floor was just an open area that would normally be used as a dance floor. We decided to place tables and chairs on the main floor, creating a more intimate dinner theater style environment. We ended up with a capacity of 800, which proved to be the perfect fit for us.

Tyler was not involved in the venue search, but we made a point to keep him in the loop so that once we had decided on a place and a date, we could jump right into ramping up the show itself. There was no question we all thought the show was great as it was. The issue was how we could promote it. I knew from our experience on the first tour that we couldn't just throw up some radio spots and expect people to show up. Tyler's name meant nothing back then so we would need some kind of hook for the promotion. No one else in his original cast had any kind of name recognition so the only option we had was to add some star power to the cast.

Tyler was not a part of this decision making process either. We would seek his input on specific names of people we were considering bringing on, but to be honest, he never really seemed all that interested. We would ask him about certain celebrities we thought we could get and, at most, he would respond with "yeah, that'd be cool" or "sounds good, let's get 'em" but he never offered any suggestions or any kind of useful feedback. He pretty much left it up to me and Nia to decide who to bring on.

I don't mean that negatively, and I don't want to imply that he was incapable or didn't care. It's just that we weren't having creative discussions on the merits of one performer versus another. We were focused on who could put butts in those seats because, even with the legitimacy of the venue, we needed something more. No matter how good your show is, you do not sell out the House of Blues, or anywhere else for that matter, by promoting a new show with a no-name writer and a no-name cast. We learned that much in Wichita and Little Rock.

Eventually we decided on a comedienne named Small Fry and a singer by the name of Ann Nesby. Small Fry wasn't exactly huge back then but she was recognizable from her work on Def Comedy Jam. Ann Nesby was the former lead singer of an R&B/Gospel group called The Sounds of Blackness. This was a fairly big "get" for us because, not only were The Sounds of Blackness big at the time, but their hit song "Change is Coming" was the closing song in the show. In addition, we added Quan Howell and Carl Pertile who had replaced Ann as the new leads with the Sounds of Blackness, giving us all three of the lead singers of that group in our show. Now, finally, we had something to promote.

There was one small problem. There was no role for Ann Nesby in the original script. This is where talent separates the good from the great. We finally had the makings of a successful promotion, but the key piece of our approach didn't have a clear role to play in the show. Well, it turns out that wasn't a problem after all. Tyler simply wrote a significant part for her to play and it turned out great. Someone of lesser talent would not have been able to do that so easily or so quickly, but Tyler Perry is not someone of lesser talent. The man is a creative genius as he has proved time and again throughout his career. The fact that we were able to use his talent in a way that specifically aided the promotion moved us one step closer to our goal. I think we could all feel it—this was coming together and it was going to be big.

Along with being creatively gifted, Tyler always had an innate vision of his place in the business and of the power of his brand. On the surface, it might be easy to come to the conclusion he was motivated by ego and I'm sure that was a part of it. But I also think he understood that if he could establish himself as a legitimate star, he would have more control. As it was, when Nia and I were putting together the radio spots, we initially wanted to remove his name from the title. In fact, we wanted to remove his name from all of the advertising. We didn't mean it as a slight to him, but we felt that since nobody knew who he was, using his name might cause more confusion than anything else. Tyler wasn't trying to hear any of that. To his credit, he was adamant that it would ALWAYS say, "Tyler Perry's I Know I've Been Changed."

In hindsight there was a certain genius to this. Making his name front and center established his brand and created the perception of him as the star. So as he moved forward with his career, he would no longer have to worry about finding star power to sell his projects, he was the star power.

Anyone familiar with Tyler's work knows he doesn't use A-list talent in his shows. He doesn't have to, and not using A-list talent means he doesn't have to pay A-list rates. He doesn't have to pay anything close to what other projects are paying for talent because he doesn't need them to sell tickets.

Of course this wasn't always the case and it damn sure wasn't the case when we did the House of Blues. We went out and got Ann Nesby because we needed her name to sell tickets and Tyler understood why it had to be done. The way he is able to conduct his business today is a direct result of the foundation we laid back then. For him to suggest he did this all on his own suggests people bought those tickets to the House of Blues to see him. He knows that's not how it happened. He wasn't anywhere near the top of that mountain yet, and he knew it. He knew he needed our help which is why he was so willing to step aside and let Nia and I make those decisions. He might not have been very involved with all the logistics required to put this thing together, but he knew damn well that a lot of work was going into making this happen, and he knew damn well who was doing it.

Now that we had a cast we could work with and the venue secured, it was time to start building the promotion. Atlanta wasn't really my town so to avoid a repeat of the Saint Louis fiasco; I reached out to Preston Elliott to buy all of our advertising. Preston was well known in the area and would be able to get the best rates for both radio and TV. He also knew exactly what we would need to be successful so I could rest easy that we were not gonna fall short because of the advertising. The best thing was that he got paid a percentage of what the stations made, so he didn't cost us anything. Finding Preston really felt like the final piece of the puzzle. He determined we would need a budget of about forty-five thousand dollars, which we of course had courtesy of our friend from Miami. Everything was in place for a successful promotion. Of course nothing in this business is ever guaranteed, but I was extremely confident. We had a great show, name talent, and a venue with some cache. Most importantly, we had the resources to get the word out.

We all worked extremely hard up to this point and were all proud of what we were able to put together. But the harsh truth is none of this would have happened, none of it, if we didn't have the money to buy that advertising. A homeless man, sleeping in his car, does not have forty-five thousand dollars to buy TV and radio ads.

He doesn't have the money to pay Ann Nesby. He doesn't have the money to rent the building or pay for insurance. A homeless person has no phone so he has no way of coordinating anything. How would he contact the cast to let them know about rehearsals or when the show was going to be? How would he coordinate load in times with the venue?

Any reasonable person can easily see that Tyler's version of what happened doesn't make sense. Unfortunately, most artists who live and breathe in the creative realm are anything but reasonable. They can't afford to be. They are people who put their lives on the line for the sake of their dreams. They are people for whom artistic expression is their only form of peace. They are people who live on hope and this is the cloth from which Tyler is cut. For him to selfishly perpetuate a fallacy solely for the sake of his image, when it would literally cost him nothing to acknowledge the truth, is a betrayal that defies logic. Anyone who has ever coordinated anything, from a wedding to a surprise birthday party, knows it would be impossible for a homeless man to pull this off by himself.

If you want to know how Tyler Perry went from being a virtual nobody to selling out the House of Blues, the answer is simple. He was able to buy $45,000 of advertising. How was he able to do that? We gambled a hundred thousand dollars of drug money without regard to our personal safety or that of our families. That is how it happened and that is what separated him from all the other talented artists out there struggling to make it.

For anyone who simply doesn't believe Tyler would have done that, I am sorry but you are being naïve. Just as naïve as anyone who thinks Tyler Perry is the only celebrity to get his start this way. For good or bad, that's the way the entertainment business works and any aspiring performer who buys into the fantasy Tyler puts out as his bio is dooming himself to failure because it doesn't happen that way. It didn't for Tyler Perry and it won't for you.

CHAPTER
13

Back in the Game

We sold out the House of Blues before opening night and all the performances exceeded even our wildest expectations. The crowd ate it up like candy and left each show wanting more. We had done it. Literally six weeks earlier we were flat on our asses broke, with no real clue how to get the show back up. Now we had six sold out performances at the House of Blues!

I made it a point to sit outside in the lobby at the end of every show and listen to the audience reactions as they left the theater. I found this was the best way to get honest feedback after a show because I would simply overhear the comments people were making to each other. I learned to be suspicious of the comments people made to me directly because, more often than not, they would try to be nice so they could avoid hurting my feelings. By just listening in on their conversations, I wouldn't have to worry about them not being honest. Plus, they didn't have any idea who I was or that I had anything to do with the show so they had absolutely no reason to filter their comments.

As good as I thought the show was, I was still overwhelmed at the positive responses I heard as people were leaving. Again, none of them knew who I was or that I was eavesdropping on their conversations, so they had no reason to lie. To say they loved it would be an understatement. This show had moved them, and I knew that was the key.

For the audience to just like it or enjoy it wasn't going to cut it. We needed to touch them enough that they would want to go home and tell their friends and family about it. If they just liked it they would tell a few friends about it, but only when asked. People don't run home and call their mother or their girlfriends and say "girl, I liked the show."

If they are touched or moved by what you are offering, that's a whole different story. That's when they start making phone calls wanting to tell people about it. It becomes their go-to topic of conversation when they go to work, meet someone new or run into old friends after church. Essentially, if you can connect with and touch your audience, they will become your publicists, sales staff and street team all rolled up in one package. And they will probably be far more effective than the so-called professionals you are paying to do the same job.

Tyler had started doing alter calls at the end of the shows, and you could tell by the way the audience reacted that the show touched them. Between the alter calls and the responses I heard as people were leaving the theater, I knew we were on our way. There was no doubt in my mind that, if done right, this show could change lives.

The most common sentiment I heard after the show was that they had never seen anything like it before. That's when

I began to take a look at our demographics and realized this wasn't exactly your typical gospel play audience. Don't get me wrong, the show was something completely beyond anything that was being done back then. But what made us stand out even more was the fact that we were able to attract a younger audience because of our marketing. We chose a venue that was considered an "it" place amongst a younger set, we cast talent that was attractive to a younger demographic and we developed spots that made the show seem cool. We gave Tyler an audience of his peers, and he completely won them over.

The key thing to remember is that we hadn't even begun to touch the traditional black theater going audience yet. Without even trying, we had started building an entirely new marketplace for black theater and this new market was 100% sold on Tyler Perry. Not only because he was unquestionably talented, but also because he was all they had. He was the only one doing stuff that spoke to them and they related to what he was presenting. Hell, when I think about it, that's the whole reason I fell in love with the show when I first saw it.

The significance of what was happening should not be dismissed. Anyone looking at the trajectory of Tyler Perry's career has to go back to those early days and see how we, almost by accident, created a whole new market for the product he was offering. We catered to a market that, even today, is dismissed by mainstream or traditional outlets.

Let's be clear. What Tyler Perry had done since 2005 is unprecedented in Hollywood. Not just so-called black Hollywood, but all of Hollywood. In the history of filmmaking, no one has ever enjoyed the success he has in his first seven films. Not Spielberg, not George Lucas, no one. This is a verifiable fact and yet he still carries with him the negative perception that he only sells to a niche audience of black women, while this may be technically true from a demographic perspective, what they don't say is that the black dollar is every bit as powerful as any other. And when concentrated on a single figure, it is even more so.

We knew we had to build an audience for Tyler back then. That was obvious because he was new, but what we didn't realize was that by skewing our marketing towards a slightly younger crowd, we were building an audience that was young enough to "grow" with him. So as he went on to bigger and better things, his audience would be able to go with him and the bond he formed with them early on, would only become stronger over time. So much so that he is now able to take them across platforms and transition from the stage to the screen and even to his own cable TV network. All of this while remaining true to his core audience, even standing up to the criticism of Spike Lee, and others, who see his work as degrading.

What Spike doesn't realize is that Tyler and his audience have done this together. It doesn't matter what anyone else thinks because he is speaking directly to them in a way they want to be spoken to. The loyalty they have for him is reciprocated in the fact that their support shields him from having to conform to anyone else's standard but theirs. He remains true to them because their dollars protect him. There aren't very many artists throughout history who can claim this kind of relationship with their audience. It didn't happen overnight, and he didn't do it all by himself, but it did happen. And he must be given credit for his part in building something that has never before been seen.

As always, Tyler and the cast were doing their thing on stage and making the audience fall in love with them. As the week went on, and the responses kept getting better, I began to realize just how big this could be. I always knew it was a good show and that there was some money to be made if it was promoted correctly. But now I was starting to see a far bigger picture. If we could tour this show nationally, we would be rich.

All the elements were in place. We had a great show, a solid cast and a budding superstar in Tyler Perry. Most importantly, we had finally figured out how to properly market the piece. Keep in mind that we sold out House of Blues before opening night, so we did not benefit from any word of mouth. Every night was an entirely brand new audience, and each night the responses kept getting better. I didn't know it at the time but we were expanding our audience with each show. They say there is no better promotion than a good performance and each night at the House of Blues was like the best 120-minute infomercial ever created. Because of the uniqueness of the venue, we were able to do some very creative things with staging, like having actors leave the stage and exit through the audience. This combined with the fact that our audience wasn't exactly theater savvy allowed us to break, or rewrite, the rules to suit our show. We were able to create a theater experience for our audience that they weren't expecting and the response was overwhelming.

I knew we needed to start thinking national tour but there was still a pretty big problem—we didn't have enough money. After expenses, I would come out of the House of Blues with about $120,000, half of which belonged to our Miami benefactor, not exactly the kind of guy you hold money from.

Plus, I still owed David $50,000; so really, I only had a rightful claim to about $10,000. Oh and I had a pregnant wife and family in Oklahoma City. As successful as we were at House of Blues, we were by no means out of the woods. Far from it.

I knew I needed more cash, but I didn't want to go back to Chico. By then, I realized how much money he probably had but, in all honesty, I wasn't comfortable dealing with him on that level. It wasn't any kind of moral judgment on my part, I just felt like if he was balling on that level, there was probably some drama that went along with being in business with him. That wasn't something I was prepared to deal with. I did manage to persuade him to roll over his initial investment in the show so I was able to hold onto his half of the profit. Still, that wasn't nearly enough to take the show national. I was stuck without more money and I knew it. What I did have now was verifiable proof that the show could sell, so I called Arthur.

The definition of insanity is to do the same thing over and over and expect a different result. Well I definitely must have been out of my mind because Arthur told me, on multiple occasions and with not a hint of hesitation that he thought the show sucked. Not only did he think it was, and I quote, "A piece of shit," but he was sure that I was a damn fool for messing with it.

When I called him about the House of Blues, hoping it would change his mind; he laughed at me and said we got lucky. Not only that, he dismissed the whole thing saying we only sold 800 tickets a night and that wasn't even close to enough to make any real money on a tour, all of which was 100% true. He reiterated how much of a fool he thought I was and told me

I needed to bring my ass home because I didn't know what the hell I was doing. By the end of the conversation, I was every bit as depressed as I was before we did the House of Blues. I wasn't about to give up because I still believed in my heart that Arthur was wrong, but I had no obvious moves to make. If this was going to happen, I was going to need a break.

"Hey Melvin, it's Preston . . ."

"What's up Preston?" I said, curious why he was calling.

"The Fox just called me . . . they had a cancellation next weekend. You want the date?" he said excitedly, obviously thinking this was big news.

"Lemme think about it and get back to you." I said after a moment of hesitation.

"Alright, let me know." He said as he hung up. I could tell he was confused by my reaction and no I'm not crazy. But the Fox and its 4,500 seats was big step up from the 800 seat House of Blues. Lastly, I got the call from Preston on a Wednesday and the opening was the next Saturday, leaving us less than two weeks to promote.

Looking back, there really wasn't anything to think about. We didn't have enough money to do anything else but a local show and, honestly, the timing was absolutely perfect. Since we had literally just closed the House of Blues two days earlier, the cast was still together and ready to go. I knew Tyler would be down because we had been talking over those two days trying to figure out where to go next so really the only question was if we would have enough time to promote.

What I didn't think of was that, unlike the House of Blues, this time we would have significant word of mouth. Because the two shows were so close together, everything was still fresh in the minds of the audience. People who felt like they missed out on the House of Blues would now have a second chance. The radio spots could be tweaked and reused and because Chico had rolled his money over, we would have plenty of money to advertise. Lastly, the venue was desperately trying to fill this opening so they gave us a really good break on the rental. This couldn't have worked out better if I had planned it. I called Preston back 15 minutes later and told him we were in. He told me how much we would need to advertise, and I told him that wouldn't be a problem. The next time I heard from Preston was when he called me two days before we opened at the Fox and told me we had sold out.

CHAPTER
14

How You Like Me Now?

While Tyler had little or nothing to do with us selling out the House of Blues, he, and the rest of the cast, had everything to do with our success at the Fox. What we had done that first week was unprecedented. To sell out a venue like the House of Blues with a new show and an unknown writer just wasn't done in a city like Atlanta where there was a ton of competition. Atlanta was, and still is, a major stop for gospel plays and many other forms of entertainment targeting the black community. Any national promoter who toured the nation with black acts would be intimately familiar with what was going on there and, after the House of Blues; we were what was going on. The only problem from their perspective was they didn't know who the hell we were, all that was about to change.

The word of mouth from House of Blues was off the charts so all we had to do was let people know of the show at the Fox and the rest took care of itself. Nine thousand seats sold in one week. That's insane when you think about where we were just 3 months before, and it was all because of how good Tyler and his show was. There was no longer a question or a doubt in any of our minds; we were definitely on our way.

The audience reaction at the Fox was every bit as good as the House of Blues. This was really good for us because there were some really big national promoters there to see the show. Preston called me before we opened at the Fox to tell me they would be there and wanted to talk to me after they saw the show. Why didn't they want to speak to Tyler? Well, even though he was the star of the show, he really wasn't anything close to what you would call a headliner. Sure, after the House of Blues, his name was ringing out in Atlanta, but it still meant less than nothing nationally. If anything, Ann Nesby and the Sounds of Blackness were our headliners. It would be years before Tyler's brand was solidly established on a national level and those promoters weren't remotely interested in building the Tyler Perry name. They wanted his show, with or without Tyler.

Yes, that is true. Tyler had licensed the show to me so technically I had the right to produce it anywhere I chose as long as he was paid his royalty as the writer. He could even stipulate that it would always be referred to as "Tyler Perry's I Know I've Been Changed," but what he couldn't do was insist I put him in the show. Because he was still an unknown outside of Atlanta, he had no leverage upon which to negotiate anything. What's more, he knew that so he never made an issue of Nia and I meeting with the promoters, and we never, for a second, considered doing the show without him. Not only did we consider him a friend, but we knew how talented he was and that the show would not be the same without him in it. Aside from all that, we had literally just been through hell to get to this point. We were in this thing together and the three of us would sink or swim with each other, or so I thought.

Things were happening now and we could all feel it. I'd love to tell you I sat back and enjoyed my moment of triumph, but honestly, I was beginning to feel like I was in over my head. That's the funny thing about success. It rarely comes when you think it will and never happens the way you planned. We've all heard the saying, "He might not come when you want Him to, but He's always right on time" right? Well right about then I wanted, no I needed, someone to tell me what to do.

See, that's one of those harsh life lessons they forget to prepare you for in school. More businesses fail because they are not prepared for success than the other way around. Your window of opportunity is small in any business, but it is especially small in the entertainment industry. So when opportunity knocks you have to be prepared. Remember how we spoke earlier about every artist wanting to have his or her moment? Well it really is just a moment. Opportunity waits for no one so if you're not ready or if you make the wrong decision and your moment passes, God only knows when, or if, the window will ever open again. Most times it doesn't and you spend the rest of your life wondering what if.

That was the kind of pressure I felt as all these big wigs were suddenly coming at me. I needed to make some decisions and those decisions wouldn't just affect me. I had Tyler, Nia, and my family, all looking to me to know what to do, but I honestly had no clue. Yeah I had big dreams and aspirations but, in reality, I was just a regular guy from Oklahoma City who didn't know the first thing about touring the country. Arthur was right.

I didn't know what the hell I was doing. But I did know someone who did . . .

"Yeah yea, I heard all about it." Arthur said as he answered the phone, knowing it was me and assuming I was calling to gloat. I was calling him from a corner in the lobby of the Fox as our second show was coming to an end.

"Arthur, man this shit is crazy. I got Dave Rubin, Joe Meachem and some lady named Mary Card from Baci all wanting to meet with me after the show. What should I do?" I'm sure he could hear the anxiety in my voice, which is probably why he took on such a calming tone.

"Tell you what, go ahead and take the meetings but don't commit to anything. Just see what they have to say, and I'll call you back."

I can't describe it really, but his approval seemed to instantly change my mindset. Just like that I went from being a scared country bumpkin, overwhelmed by the bright lights of the big city, to being my normal cocky self. It felt good and I actually started to let myself enjoy my moment just a little bit.

"Alright cool," I said, feeling confident now that I knew Arthur would help me, "One more thing before I let you go though . . ."

"What's that," he said

"How you like me now NIGGA!!!" Come on, you know I had to gloat a little bit.

CHAPTER

15

We've Only Just Begun

"Hello?" I said groggily as I answered the phone still half asleep from the night before. Nia and I went out after our meetings with the promoters to have a little celebration so, needless to say, I wasn't in my best mental state at that moment. I half expected it to be Tyler calling, wanting to know what was going on.

"Here's what we gonna do Melvin Childs . . ."

"Arthur?" I interrupted, realizing who it was.

"Yeah, now wake your ass up. We got work to do."

"I'm up man," I lied as I sat up on Nia's sofa.

"What's the move?"

"You meet with the promoters?" he asked

"Yeah, we talked for a minute but I didn't commit to anything with anybody just like you said."

"Good."

"So what's up? What we gonna do?" I asked anxiously.

"We gonna do this shit ourselves Melvin Childs."

And with that, the die was cast. Arthur agreed to come to Atlanta and function as our tour manager.

To save money, he would stay at Nia's place while I would head back home to Oklahoma City to try and fix things with my wife. I had been in Atlanta for months now, and it was time for me to take my ass home and see about my family. And now that I had Arthur on board to watch my back, I didn't have to stay on top of every little detail. He knew the business better than I did so I could take a step back and relax a little bit.

My homecoming was as you might expect. Nobody was very happy with me, especially my wife, so there was no welcome home Melvin sign waiting for me in the living room. I tried, as best I could, to justify being gone for so long, but she wasn't trying to hear any of it. Being as young, dumb, and self-absorbed, as I was, I thought the fact that I was able to pay her back all of the money she leant me would help smooth things over. Wrong answer.

Not that the money didn't help. We weren't, and still aren't, rich people so being able to put a few thousand dollars in our bank account was a big deal. The problem was it didn't begin to address the root of our issues. I had placed Tyler and his show above my very own family in terms of my priorities. And no this was not done out of any great sense of loyalty to Tyler. I did consider him a friend but of course, but I had my own selfish reasons for doing what I did.

In my defense, I always had my eye on the financial benefits my family could experience if I were to become successful. My problem was I never calculated the damage I was doing by not being around. No matter how much money I made, it could never make up for the time I lost chasing this dream. I wanted, desperately, to be a player in the entertainment business and, from the day we first met, I knew that Tyler could help me achieve that.

So yes, I placed his needs on equal, and sometimes superior, footing to my own or that of my family. Was that the right thing to do? Of course it wasn't. But I frankly didn't know that at the time. Back then, I just assumed everything would work itself out and my family, for as much pain as I caused them by being gone, would one day, benefit from my insane ambition.

As it turns out, I couldn't have been more wrong. Don't misunderstand me, a lot of people ended up reaping the benefits of my betting everything I owned on an unknown playwright from New Orleans, it's just that none of them are in my immediate family. In fact, of all the people who ended up benefiting from my belief in Tyler and his talent, the two people who gained the most I have absolutely no relationship with today. One of them is Tyler Perry himself, and the other is Arthur Primas.

Baci was a huge promotion company back then that controlled several major black markets across the U.S. Arthur set us up with them to finance the tour with a fifty thousand dollar weekly guarantee for expenses plus an additional ten thousand dollars per week for Nia and myself as producers.

What this means is that, regardless of how the show did in any given city, we would be guaranteed sixty thousand dollars for the week, fifty of which had to be used for expenses. The remaining ten would go in our pockets. So, essentially, as long as we kept our weekly expenses below fifty thousand dollars, we would have no risk. Baci would assume all the risk involved in the project—at least theoretically.

After our guarantees, Baci would own fifty percent of the show, and Nia and I would have the remaining fifty percent. As for Tyler, since he was not a producer, he wouldn't own any piece of the show itself. He would be paid a percentage of gross ticket sales as the writer.

The standard royalty rate for a new writer was three percent of the gross. Basically that means the writer gets three cents for every dollar of ticket sales. The gross part is key because it guarantees your money. Since your royalty comes off the top, you are going to get paid regardless of how the show itself is doing. The promoters and producers could be getting their asses kicked but, if you are the writer, that ain't your problem. Your money comes to you or the contract is void and you take back ownership of your piece. This is the standard arrangement for a writer of a touring production—only Tyler wanted more.

While we were busy planning and scheduling, Tyler went and hired himself an agent. His name was Ron Gwiazda and when it came time to finalize Tyler's deal, he told us we had to talk to this guy. Now I had some experience dealing with talent and agents, so talking to Ron wasn't a huge deal. It's just that Tyler and I had the kind of relationship to where we could deal directly with each other. Or at least that's what I thought. I didn't have a problem with him having an agent, it just felt really unnecessary for what we were doing. I think even Tyler himself would admit it was a little premature. Especially considering he ended up firing the guy.

At any rate Ron started the negotiation off by demanding a seven percent royalty for Tyler, which is unheard of for a no-name writer. And outside of Atlanta, Tyler Perry was still very much a no-name. As the entity assuming all the risk, I would have to run the request by Baci. They of course told me to tell Tyler to go screw himself. He was getting his three percent and that was it. There was going to be no negotiation because, as we discussed earlier, Tyler had no leverage upon which to negotiate. Of course, Ron had other ideas.

He continued to hold fast to his seven percent demand even though we told him it wasn't going to happen. I tried reaching out directly to Tyler, but he would only say I had to work this out with Ron. At the same time, I had Baci in my ear telling me we had to remount the show and build a real set. The sheet and steps we had been using would absolutely not fly for a national tour and so I would have to pay for a set to be built. When I asked how much that would cost, they told me about $100,000 should do it. I had the money because we held onto all the money we made from the Fox, but still that was a big chunk of change, and I was getting tired of being the only one on the damn team writing checks. On top of all that, Baci was getting impatient and wanted to know why Tyler hadn't signed his deal yet, and Ron could have cared less. He was going to stand on seven percent—period.

So here I was, about to shell out a hundred thousand dollars for a set for his show and he was making me deal with this asshole Ron who had no idea what the hell he was talking about. I went off, and called Ron everything but a child of God. I cussed him up one side of the phone and down the other until he hung up and called Tyler to tell him how unprofessional I was. Tyler finally called me himself and asked if we could do three percent for the first seven months of the tour and then kick it up to five percent after that. I was able to sell that to Baci and so we were finally good to go.

I could say that the whole Tyler, agent negotiation fiasco was just an interesting anecdote, but it was more than that. Any time you try to mix friendship with business you run the risk of damaging one or the other. I've said many times in this book that I considered Tyler to be a friend, and I meant that sincerely. Some of you may have a difficult time believing that but I imagine that's because you see him only as the powerful media mogul he has become. Well, he wasn't famous or wealthy back then—he was just a regular dude, and we had been through a lot during that time. In that context, it makes perfect sense that I saw him as a friend. I cannot speak for him so I can't say he saw me in the same light. I do think he would acknowledge we had a personal relationship that transcended business. Whether he would call it a friendship or not, I don't know.

What I do know is that the whole thing with the agent was really a precursor of many things to come. Since Nia and I owned the biggest piece of the show, we were in charge. And since Tyler was being paid as a writer and performer, that technically made me his boss. The friendship or relationship or whatever you choose to call it, was strained right from the beginning because I was the one who had to tell him no. Of course I was stuck in the middle between Ron the asshole agent and Baci, but Tyler didn't see it like that. To him, I was the one calling the shots even though he was the one with all the talent. That didn't sit well with him and things were about to get worse.

Baci decided we should build the set and remount the show in Baltimore, Maryland. Baltimore was one of the major markets they controlled so, if we built it there, we could start the tour there as well. It seemed to make sense, even though it was gonna be expensive. By the end of the remounting process, I was out of money. Between the set and all the expenses of putting everyone up in Baltimore, we had gone through every dime we made at the Fox, plus some. Our only saving grace was the sixty thousand dollar guarantee we had coming. The fifty thousand would ensure us we would be able to keep the show on the road while we recouped the money spent remounting, and the remaining ten would allow us to eat.

I know to most people reading this, ten thousand dollars per week is a lot of money, and it is. But keep in mind, I had to split that with Nia, so it was really more like five thousand. In addition we had to start paying Chico back and I still owed David his fifty thousand dollars. I was not, by any means rolling off that ten grand. At best, that would keep me afloat until our royalty started to kick in, and that's where my eyes were set.

Things started off very well. Baltimore was a huge success but we didn't get to participate financially because we owed Baci so much money from the remounting that we had to do those dates just to get back to zero. At least that's what Arthur told us, and we had no reason not to believe him.

The next city was Richmond, Virginia and that was a hit as well. This time we did get to participate and all the money came out as it should. We were officially on our first national tour and things couldn't have started off any better with one exception.

By the second week of the tour, Tyler decided he didn't want to ride to and from the show with the rest of the cast anymore. He asked me to get him a town car. Now we were doing full eight show weeks in each city, and we needed two vans to get the cast to and from the hotel and to the venue, which cost more than seven hundred dollars each week. Now he wanted to add another twelve hundred per week on top of that for one car. For one person no way!

I didn't tell him no at first. I just kept putting him off, telling him we would talk about it. Keep in mind we were only in week two of the tour, and I was still trying to recoup all the money I invested in the remounting. I was doing everything I could to control our expenses, but Tyler wouldn't let it go. So I went to Arthur and asked him what I should do.

"Tell that nigga NO Melvin Childs!" he said unequivocally. "You the producer so he ain't callin" no shots around here. You got to control these expenses. Tell his ass he can ride in the van like every damn body else."

So that's what I did and needless to say, Tyler was not very happy. He immediately stopped speaking to me. I mean not even hello, and by the third week, he insisted on not riding in the vans anymore. So, since I wouldn't provide him a car of his own, he literally started bumming rides. I'm not kidding. You can ask anyone in the cast from that show. We all saw the same thing. I don't know who these people were or how he knew them. I just know that we would be in front of the hotel, with everyone in the van ready to go, and Tyler would be standing there waiting for his ride to show up. Same thing after the show.

This went on for a few weeks until I relented. I couldn't have the star of the damn show bumming rides from the audience. That was ridiculous, and there was a safety issue as well. Those first few cities were very successful which means we had large audiences. It wouldn't be a stretch for any one of those people to assume Tyler, as the star of the show, had it going on financially. I, of course, knew he didn't but that's not the point. I didn't want to take the chance that something would happen, so I got him his stupid car.

When he got what he wanted, he started speaking to me again. For me though, the damage was already done. He had acted like a spoiled child when I didn't give him what he wanted and I, consequently, lost a lot of respect for him. What made it even worse, in my eyes, was the level of disrespect he showed for me as a person. For him to act a fool over a damn car when we had just gotten out on the road, and we were still trying to make sure everything was working properly was beyond selfish. It was downright disrespectful. What I had done for him was nothing short of amazing. Less than six months ago I was paying for him to stay in a two hundred dollar a week hotel and now we were out on the road, performing in front sold out houses, and to top it off, he was getting paid very well to do something he loved to do. I had done nothing but right by Tyler and the least I would have expected is for him to show some appreciation by not acting like an ass because I didn't provide him with freaking limo service. Then for me to give him the car and for him not to apologize for the way he carried on was unforgivable. Our relationship was never the same after that.

16

Let the Games Begin

From the beginning, Arthur had very little respect for Tyler and he didn't think he was all that talented. See, Arthur was an old school promoter so he had little or no respect for talent in general. Success or failure in this business would come as a result of the promotion. Talent was secondary, if that, at least that was the old school way of thinking. He figured, with enough money behind you, anybody could look like a star. And in a sense he was right. If you say anything loudly or often enough, somebody, somewhere will start to believe it. And with enough money, you could say whatever you wanted as often and as loudly as you wanted.

So while I saw Tyler as a special talent, Arthur just saw him as another pain in the ass actor who thought his shit didn't stink. He was constantly on me to keep him in line, mostly about his spending. I was the producer and it was my job to control our expenses. Tyler, on the other hand, was living his dream so he was only concerned with setting everything up the way he saw it in his head. To an extent, that was understandable considering how long he had struggled trying to make it.

When you are a struggling artist, sometimes the only thing that keeps you going is that vision of how everything is going to be when you finally get your break. So for those lucky few who hit the lottery and get discovered, there is a tendency to spend those first few months and years trying to recreate the picture you've been seeing in your head for all that time.

Unfortunately, more often than not, that picture you've painted is not based on reality. You see yourself in a big house, or flying first class or riding in limos everywhere you go because that's how you have defined your success. And after getting bullied and ridiculed and told that you would never make it, you want to wear your success like a badge of honor. These are the things you've sacrificed, cried and sweated for and no one should have the right to keep them from you anymore.

What you don't realize is that it's all a fantasy created by some promoter or advertising agency. The trappings of wealth are just that—a trap. A massive shell game designed to recycle whatever money you make right back into the system. And Tyler fell right into the trap.

One thing was clear from the beginning, Tyler could spend some money. This was especially hard for me to deal with because this was the same person I saw eating peanut butter and jelly sandwiches when we were on the road the first time. Now I was looking at five and six hundred dollar room service bills. I gave him the money to pay his cast when he didn't have it, and now he was sticking me up for car service because he was too good to ride for ten minutes to and from the venue with the cast. The resentment was absolutely building up inside me and Arthur fueled it even more. It was always "Fuck that nigga, Melvin Childs! You the producer, tell his punk ass no!" or "Melvin Childs you think that chicken shit nigga thinking about you?! HELL NO! Tell him to kiss your ass!"

That's what Arthur was putting in my ear as I was seeing our expenses grow out of control. I never begrudged Tyler making his money, I was honestly happy for him. What I did have a problem with was his total lack of respect for my situation. The fifty thousand dollar guarantee went towards the cast salaries and all of our travel expenses. After that, there wasn't much of anything left over, so Tyler's twelve hundred dollar per week town car would have to come directly out of my pocket. And remember, I had to split my producers guarantee with Nia, pay Chico and David back, and I had a family at home. There was literally almost nothing left, and I told Tyler this, but he didn't care.

Keep in mind Tyler's money was guaranteed every week. He got paid regardless of how the show was doing so I saw it as a personal slap in the face for him to come at me like this considering how many times I had been there for him. Say what you want about me or Tyler or anything I've written in this book, but at some point we are no longer celebrities or promoters or fans. At some point we are all just people, and when we get to that place right is right and wrong is wrong and Tyler was wrong for that shit.

None of that mattered. He wanted what he wanted and he didn't want to hear anything else. My problems were not his problems, that much he made clear and his attitude, together with Arthur's constant instigating, was starting to piss me off. I'm not even saying that he should have always agreed with every decision I made, but based solely on what we'd been through together, I expected him to handle our disagreements with a certain amount of respect. Obviously, he didn't see things the same as I did.

Arthur ran the show for us on the road. He was the tour manager, so technically he worked for us however, because of our relationship, he never really felt like he had to answer to me or to Nia. For the first few weeks, everything was cool. The show was doing well, everybody was making money, and of course, when the money is flowing, everybody is your friend. I had started to pay David back and was even able to send some money home. We weren't exactly getting rich, but things were going well up until we hit Miami.

We got killed in Miami. It wasn't anybody's fault. The advertising was good, we had some really good promotions going on, but it just didn't work as well there as in the cities before. This is what happens when you tour the country with a new act. You are going to have to absorb some losses. Miami was the first city we lost money in, and it wouldn't be the last. What made Miami unique was something else—Baci wasn't there.

Now Arthur had set up this entire tour, and he sold Nia and I on Baci as the promoter of record. They were a huge company back then and we felt like, as long as we had their backing, we would have more than a fighting chance in any city. And we had negotiated the guarantees with them, so even if we didn't do well, we would still have some money coming in.

What he didn't tell us was that Baci was never on board to do all the cities in the first place. Even worse, apparently Arthur had a falling out with Mary and some of the other people from the company back in Baltimore and so Baci pulled out of most of the cities that they were originally contracted to promote. Why does any of this matter? Well, our guarantees were negotiated with Baci. No Baci, no guarantee.

This went way beyond Tyler and his town car. The main purpose of the guarantee was to ensure we could get the show from city to city even if we took some losses. Without that, we would have to come up with the money ourselves, and we just didn't have it. Arthur had put us in this position by not being upfront about the situation with Baci. Nia was pissed, and she had every right to be. She wanted to fire Arthur, but I wasn't having any of that. I knew he should have told us what was going on with the promoters but it was too late to worry about any of that. We had to come up with the money to get to the next city and the only solution Arthur had was to not pay Nia and myself. He tried to make us feel better about the situation by offering to repay us in the next city.

Neither of us was happy as you can imagine, but we sucked it up and dealt with it. To be honest, we didn't have much of a choice in the matter. The money had to come from somewhere or we wouldn't have a show. Speaking for myself, there was no way I could afford to shut the show down. That income was all I had at that point so I desperately needed that show to stay out, even if that meant getting shorted in Miami. I figured as long as I could make it to the next week there would, hopefully, be some money for me. A least that's what I hoped, but hope is a funny thing.

CHAPTER

17

You Done Lost Your Mind

Things went from bad to worse. After Miami, the tour was completely hit or miss. We would do very well in some cities, but completely bomb in others. The problem was, without any guarantee, we had to cover all the losses ourselves. And the losses were huge, which meant that Nia and I were hardly ever getting paid anything at all. Fortunately we had worked out a merchandising deal with Tyler for T-shirts and posters and things like that, which allowed us to have enough money to eat.

On top of that, I was having more and more problems with Tyler. Now that he was experiencing some success he, naturally, wanted to have more control. Well, I was still the producer so I was still calling the shots, and this became a bigger and bigger issue for us as we were on the road. I was hardly getting paid at this point so my sole focus in life was controlling our expenses any way I could. I confronted Tyler about his room service bills on several occasions, and he would throw a tantrum every time. It got to the point that I didn't care anymore.

He could cuss and pout all he wanted but I was the damn producer and so, if he couldn't listen to reason and act like an adult I would have to treat his ass like a child, which is exactly what I did one day.

We were flying to Columbia, South Carolina out of Chicago and the only airline that flew direct was Southwest. As many of you know, Southwest does not do any kind of reserved seating, its all first come first serve, at least it was back then. Anyway, Tyler is about six foot seven so he always requested we reserve him an exit row seat whenever we flew. Well, Southwest doesn't reserve seats, so by the time he boarded the plane there were no exit row seats left. Tyler went OFF!

I was getting to the airport late, so I wasn't on the plane when it first started. I got a call from Belinda, our company manager, letting me know that Tyler wasn't happy with his seat and wanted to know what we were going to do to fix it. As stressed as I was with everything going on around the show and as broke as I was, I damned sure wasn't about to put up with any diva shit from Tyler that day. By the time I got on the plane I already had an attitude, but I tried to maintain my cool, at first.

"What's going on?" I asked as I walked onto the plane, knowing full well what the situation was. Tyler had gone back to the front of the plane when he couldn't find an exit row seat and Belinda, our company manager was trying to calm him down.

"Shit is fucked up Melvin, I told y'all I needed an exit row seat and y'all . . ."

"Hold up dawg," I interrupted, trying to maintain some semblance of cool. The plane was packed, and it wasn't all our people so, to be honest, as much as I wanted to blast him, I was trying to avoid a scene. "You know we can't reserve seats Tyler. What you want me to do?"

"Fuck that! Y'all should have been more prepared than this. I'm the star of this goddamned show and y'all don't know how to treat me. I need a damn exit row seat!" he said as he was making his way toward the back of the plane as if to show me how uncomfortable he would be in a regular seat. My blood was literally boiling. It took everything in me not to go off on him, but again, there were a lot of people on the plane and I wanted to avoid a scene. I tried, one last time, to reason with him.

"Tyler you need to calm your ass down. There's nothing I can do dawg. The exit row seats are gone. Ain't nothing I can do!"

"Fuck you Melvin, this is fucked up! I'm the star of this goddamned show and y'all better learn how to treat me."

Honestly, he kept on talking, but I didn't really hear anything after "y'all better learn how to treat me." That sounded like a threat and that was it for me. It was bad enough I was literally going broke trying to keep this show on the road, but now this ungrateful asshole thought he could talk to me like I was a kid? Oh hell no.

"FUCK YOU MOTHERFUCKER!" I said as I interrupted his tantrum.

This was in front of the entire cast so they were all shocked to see somebody talk to Tyler in this way. I didn't care at this point; he had crossed the line as far as I was concerned. "I'm the one out here sacrificing so that your ass can get paid every week so I don't wanna hear shit about being the goddamned star of no goddamn show!"

I was getting increasingly heated with every word. I obviously had a lot of pent up frustration inside which was about to come out, regardless of the consequences.

"The only reason you HAVE a damn show is because of me so you either gonna sit your ass down on this plane or you gonna find your own way to South Carolina."

Anyone who knows Tyler knows he is not a fighter, at least not in a physical sense. Even so, he is a very prideful person so there was no way he was just going to let me have the last word, especially in front of his cast.

"Fuck you motherfucker." He said, trying to stand up for himself. "Y'all need to get this shit together." By this time, the flight attendant had come to the back of the plane and told us we needed to sit down. Chris Locklear, who was sitting on an aisle seat tried to defuse the situation by offering Tyler his seat. But Tyler ignored him and kept cussing me out. "I'm the star of this show and . . ."

I was done talking. "No, Chris sit your ass down." I said, looking past Tyler, at Chris. The only two seats left were a middle seat and a window. I looked directly at Tyler in a way that made sure he knew what happened next was up to him. "Tyler, you gonna sit your ass in that seat right there."

He had two choices at that point. Sit down or man up, and he sat down and pouted all the way to South Carolina. Now, to be fair, I'm not much of a fighter myself. But, as a man, there is a difference between being able to fight and being willing to fight. Growing up, every young man learns that the true coward is never the person that loses the fight. The punk is the person who is afraid to stand up for himself.

It's been well documented that Tyler has been bullied in his life and that day on the plane, maybe for the first time, he was trying to assert himself as a man. But in that moment, for whatever reason, he wasn't willing to take it there. He backed down and, what's worse, he did it in front of his cast. I made him look weak in front of the only people in his life that made him feel powerful.

Looking back, I do feel bad about the way I handled that situation. Bad enough that I would probably apologize to Tyler if we were to ever talk about it. In hindsight, I can see that Tyler was not challenging me in a way that warranted that kind of response. Was he wrong for coming at me the way he did? Yes he was. But I was just as wrong for purposely escalating the situation. It's just that I had allowed so much frustration to build up inside me that it, unfortunately, had gotten to the point where I could no longer control it. Consequently when I saw him that day I blew up.

The harsh reality is I wasn't all that angry with Tyler. True, he was out of control with his spending, but the person I was most frustrated with was myself. I had given up everything to get this show on the road and it just wasn't working out like I thought it would. From the beginning, I figured if I could get this show up, in front of the right audience, they would love it and I would be set. I was only half right. The audience, no matter how small or large, loved the show just about everywhere we went. Unfortunately applause doesn't pay the bills. You need cash to do that and even though we were getting applause everywhere we went, I was still going broke. There was something wrong with this picture I thought. I just couldn't figure out what it was, at least not at first. Looking back, it's amazing I didn't see it coming . . .

18

I Never Saw It Coming

Each betrayal begins with trust.
—Phish

When we finished up at the House of Blues we knew we wanted to tour the country. The problem was money. Or lack thereof. Even as we wrapped up the Fox we didn't have nearly enough money for a national tour, and we knew it. What we did have was the show. Baci and the big promotion companies had the resources to tour the country. What they didn't have was the show. So we made a deal.

Baci would pay for the tour, by way of their guarantee. We, meaning Nia and myself, would provide the show and we would split what came back 50/50. This was good deal for Baci because they knew the show would play well in their markets, and it was a good deal for us because we needed their money to fund the tour. It was the kind of deal that made sense for everybody. So what went wrong?

As it turns out, while Nia and I were starving, Arthur was doing quite well for himself. He was being paid a salary of $2,000 per week for being our tour manager, which is what we had all agreed to. What we didn't realize at the time however was that, with Baci out of the deal, Arthur just assumed their 50% ownership of the show. So, in other words, he went from being an employee to being an equal partner in the deal without ever discussing it with anyone. He never discussed this with either Nia or myself because he knew there was no way in hell we would have ever agreed to it. He had nothing to offer! The only reason we gave Baci 50% was because they had assumed 100% of the risk by paying for the tour. Arthur, on the other hand, was broke. That's why, when he went to Atlanta, he was sleeping on Nia's couch.

This was all bad. Don't get me wrong; we weren't losing in every city. The show was still doing very well in certain markets and breaking even in others. But with no guarantee, whatever money Nia and I thought we would have coming was always, at best, short. Arthur controlled everything so he would tell us our money had to be used to cover previous losses or that he had to hold onto it to protect against any future losses. Essentially we became our own guarantee, which makes absolutely no sense considering we knew from the beginning that we didn't have that kind of money. That's why we were willing to license half of the show to someone who did. That's the standard way these deals are structured and Arthur knew that. I know he knew that because that's exactly what he was doing to pay for the rest of the tour. Only now, with Baci out of the picture, he was selling MY half of the show to anyone he could find with enough money to fund the dates.

I didn't see any of this coming. Arthur was more than just my friend; he was my mentor. He was like a father to me, and I brought him into this deal even though he had done nothing but bad-mouth the project from day one. I brought him into this deal even though I knew his reputation was shady. Was that a good decision? Obviously not, but in fairness to myself, I had never been anything, but good to Arthur and his family so I didn't think there was any way in hell he would steal from me. I was wrong. Not only did he steal from me, he had been setting me up all along.

Arthur had no business owning half of anything and he knew that, which is why he made sure he never gave us all the money we were owed, even when things went well. Remember, Arthur technically worked for us, so we could have fired his ass at any time. To prevent that, he needed to keep us broke. As long as we didn't have enough money to fund any of the dates ourselves, we would need to keep him out there wheeling and dealing on our behalf just to keep the show from shutting down. Of course we didn't know he was wheeling and dealing with our half of the show but, in all honesty, it wouldn't have mattered if we did.

Against Nia's wishes, I ceded all control to Arthur from the very beginning. I even went so far as to talk him up to Tyler just to make sure he was comfortable with Arthur running things. I never told Tyler any of the things Arthur used to say behind his back because I needed him to trust Arthur as much as he trusted me. Arthur was my guy, so I always thought of him as being on my team. If Tyler trusted him then, by default, I would always have a line of communication to Tyler, even as the relationship was strained from the little dust ups we had out on the road.

What I didn't anticipate was Arthur using all of that to his advantage. While I was out there fighting with Tyler, Arthur was going behind my back telling Tyler how I didn't know what I was doing. Since I was the one who had to tell Tyler no all the time, it was easy for Arthur to ease his way into Tyler's good graces by just co-signing all the things Tyler was saying about me after I would tell him he couldn't do something.

Like the time Tyler wanted to fire a backup singer for something that happened on the road. This particular singer was openly gay and apparently he had hooked up with someone in a hotel we were staying at. When Tyler found out, he immediately wanted to fire him because, in his words, "He didn't stand for that kind of activity and didn't want that representing him or his show." Well I looked past the obvious hypocrisy of those words and told him no, I wasn't going to fire the guy. Not only did I see it as none of my business what a grown man did in his private time, but this particular singer was the lowest paid person on the tour. To replace him, we would have had to find someone new and pay them more. As broke as I was, there was NO way that was gonna happen. I wasn't even trying to think about it. Of course Tyler wasn't happy about it, but there was nothing he could do. Nothing besides complain to anyone who would listen and Arthur has always been a great listener.

Arthur would co-sign all of Tyler's complaints about me, while at the same time egging me on to tell Tyler to sit down and shut up. He was working both sides of the street from the very beginning because he had already figured out what I was too stupid to see, that the real opportunity with Tyler was gonna be his next show.

All the losses we were taking on the road were unavoidable. The natural growing pains you go through when you are breaking a new artist. Both Tyler and his show were new and, because of that, we were going to struggle in certain markets. With the Baci money, that wasn't a big deal. Without it, there was NO reason we should have played some of those markets. The risk was simply too great and we didn't have the money to cover any of the losses. But Arthur didn't care about that. He was using our money to introduce Tyler to those new markets, so that he could bring him back to those places and make money the next time around. He knew, based on the audience reaction that he could go back to any one of those cities and kill. He was using the first show, MY SHOW, to set up the next one. All he had to do was get Nia and me out of the deal and he had been trying to do that since the House of Blues.

CHAPTER

19

How Could I Have Been So Stupid?

Arthur knew we were onto something when I called him after the House of Blues run. That whole "y'all just got lucky" thing was just an act. If Baci and Joe Meachem and the other major national promoters heard about what we did in Atlanta, you can bet your ass that Arthur did as well. The only reason he acted like he wasn't interested was to see if I would let it die so that he could swoop in and take it out from under me right then. When I didn't fall into that trap, he was stuck, until I called him from the Fox. That gave him the opening he needed. All he had to do was change tactics.

You have no idea how difficult it is for me to write these words. I thought the world of this man and his family. So to admit that I was never anything more than a mark to him goes far beyond humiliation. How dumb must I have been to not see it? Why was I so pathetically desperate to replace what I had lost with my father?

Pathetic is a good word. That's how I felt for years anytime I would think about how I helped Arthur set me up. Every time I would be struggling to pay the bills or have to tell my kids they couldn't have something they might have needed, I thought back to what he took from me, and how I let him do it.

He knew I trusted him with everything so taking control of the financials would be the easy part. The real trick would be to get close enough to Tyler, which turned out to be just as easy since I basically did that for him.

I was so confident in my relationship with Arthur that I went out of my way to talk him up to Tyler, and everyone else on the team. I made it seem like Arthur was the best in the business, figuring that, since he was my close personal friend, everyone would take me more seriously if they thought I knew a major player. I have no idea why I felt that way, but I did and a large part of me is embarrassed to look back and admit how dumb I was. The fact that I was so insecure as to think I needed to put on a front for a group of people I was paying is a whole new level of stupid.

Yes it was definitely a front because, in reality, Arthur was anything but a major player. He was a 50 something year old man, sitting on his ass doing nothing when I brought him into the deal. He was just as broke as the day I met him and I essentially handed him a winning lottery ticket. I don't regret it because, based on the relationship I thought we had, I would do it again. The man was like my family so of course I was going to bring him in on something like this. Unfortunately for me, those feelings were anything but mutual.

From the beginning Arthur made it a habit to just agree with whatever Tyler said, at least to his face. Whenever Tyler wasn't around Arthur couldn't stop talking about how much of an asshole he was. When he was with Tyler though, it was a different story all together. I told you earlier that Arthur can be VERY charming, and he was all that plus some when it came to Tyler. Arthur also knew that, in my position of producer, I would have to be the one to make all the unpopular decisions. The situation couldn't have been more perfect for him. He got to sit back and be the cool uncle, always lending a sympathetic ear and telling the star of the show what he wanted to hear. While I was the asshole dad, telling the same star that the rules applied to him just like they apply to everybody else and that he couldn't do whatever he wanted.

Eventually he started implying I didn't know what I was doing. And since I had made it seem like he was the best thing since sliced bread, Tyler had no reason not to believe him. Once Tyler started to buy into that line of thinking, the final piece of Arthurs puzzle was in place. Tyler now wanted me gone every bit as much as Arthur did, he just had to find a way to cut me loose. Not to worry, Uncle Arthur had a plan in place for that as well.

In all honesty, cutting ties with me would have been easy enough to do without any drama. I was only licensed to do the one show and Tyler was under NO obligation to license any other show to me. He and Arthur could have gone off and done whatever they wanted after we wrapped our tour and Tyler wouldn't have owed me a penny. There was one small problem; they didn't have the money. As it turns out, Uncle Arthur had a plan for that too . . .

CHAPTER

20

Damn, That Was Slick

Houston is one of the cities with a reputation as a place where you can make a lot of money. The demographics and economics are ideal, meaning there is a large population of employed black people. The advertising rates are reasonable and, most importantly, there were venues that have a prestige all their own. This was critical if you were breaking a new act.

Arthur had scheduled it as the last stop on our tour specifically for these reasons. I never questioned the timing because it made sense to me that we would want to end on a high note. This would also allow for us to end the tour with some resources, namely money, in place to either remount the show or do something else. Arthur knew exactly what he was doing.

We had scheduled a two-week hiatus before the Houston dates. By this time, the show was still going well creatively, but the finances were an absolute mess. Nia and I hardly ever got paid, and when we did it didn't come close to what we were owed. Arthur always had an excuse but, by that time, both Nia and I were convinced he was ripping us off. In fairness, Nia started questioning things long before I did. I resisted believing it for a long time, but by the time we were getting ready for Houston, even I couldn't deny it any longer. It was as obvious as the day is long that Arthur was getting over on us.

Arthur kept us in the dark when it came to anything to do with money. Just about the only thing he ever let us see were the invoices he created that showed us where all of our money was supposedly going. It was all complete bullshit, but by the time we started to realize it, we were in no position to do anything about it. Because Arthur controlled the finances, we had no money to make any moves on our own. Also, he had made all the side deals with all the various promoters after Baci left so, if we fired him, we ran the risk of having to shut the show down. There was also the Tyler issue.

By this point on the tour, Arthur had solidified his relationship with Tyler. Firing Arthur would have probably meant losing Tyler, especially when I was the one who told Tyler how great Arthur was in the first place. We were stuck with Arthur, at least for the time being, but I had every intention of dealing with his ass once we finished up in Houston. I knew now that he would, in fact, steal from me just like he would anyone else. What I didn't realize was just how far he would go with it, and I was about to find out.

As we were getting ready to leave for our two-week hiatus, I stopped by Arthur's room to pick up my money for that past week. As usual, it was significantly short, but I was broke so any little bit was very much needed. Besides I had started to pay attention to the numbers, at least those I had access to, and knew that Houston was shaping up nicely. A successful two week run there would be exactly what the doctor ordered.

Arthur and I shared a ride to the airport. This is when he set the last remaining piece of his plan into motion.

"Look here Melvin, I'm telling you right now, you and Nia ain't participating in this Houston date."

"What?" I said incredulously. To be honest, he was so bold with his statement that it caught me off guard. I mean, I knew he had been playing me for a sucker for months but this dude must have really thought I was crazy.

"What the hell you mean we ain't participating?"

"Man I got too many bills to cover and I still need to get my . . ."

You ever listen to somebody and know they are lying to you? And then when you make eye contact with them you realize that they know you know they're lying? Well that's what was happening. Every word coming out of Arthur's mouth right then was a damn lie, and he knew that I knew it. I almost think he was embarrassed by it, which should have been my first clue. Arthur had been smoothly lying and manipulating me for months now, so why would was this time so clumsy?

It was clumsy because it was just a diversion. He knew damn well he didn't have the authority to kick us out of the Houston dates. Hell, he knew that he had NO authority at all. He also knew there was no way in hell I was going to just walk away because he said so. If anything, even him mentioning it would make me pay that much more attention so that I could ensure Nia and I were paid correctly.

"You might as well save that bullshit dawg," I interrupted, almost laughing. "I ain't tryin' to hear none of that bullshit you talking about."

That pretty much shut the conversation down and I honestly thought that was going to be the end of it. It wasn't until months later that I realized what he was really doing. He was trying to start an argument. Why? So he would have a reason to not answer my calls for the rest of that week.

We went home on a Sunday and since our agreement was to pay Tyler his royalty every Tuesday, I started calling Arthur, looking for Tyler's money, on Monday morning. No response . . .

Monday afternoon, I called again. No response . . .

Monday night, I called a few more times. No response . . .

Tuesday passes, then Wednesday and Thursday . . . not a word from Arthur. Friday comes along and I get a letter from Tyler's new agent. I open the envelope and find a cease and desist notice informing me that Nia and I are in breach of our contract with Tyler, rendering our licensing agreement invalid effective immediately. The reason? Failure to pay royalties.

21

See You Later, Bye

The shit's chess, it ain't checkers . . .
—Alonzo Harris

While Arthur had been playing me like a yoyo for months, he definitely saved his best move for last. By holding back Tyler's money he was able to remove me from the deal, and set things up so that he could keep 100% of all the proceeds in Houston. Do I think Tyler was in on it? Yes, of course he was. I know I can't prove it, but think about it. Why would he continue to do business with Arthur if he was really upset about not getting paid? Arthur was, supposedly, my right hand man so why get rid of me and keep him?

Additionally, this wasn't the first time on the tour that he was paid late. Why take this action now? And most importantly, this is the key . . . the tour was over anyway! Houston was the last city and Tyler was under no obligation to work with me ever again. So what was the point of sending me a cease and desist letter when the tour was already over? The answer had to be money.

Remember how Arthur was selling my half of the show to promoters to pay our expenses and keeping the other half for himself? Well in some cities, Arthur made himself the promoter. Meaning he would license 50% of the show to himself, use the money he held back from Nia and I to pay expenses, and keep 100% of what came back from the box office. Yes, that is true. As ridiculous as it sounds, Nia and I were actually funding our own show in some cities, and Arthur was keeping all the proceeds. And he was doing this without any contractual authority whatsoever. We never signed any kind of deal with Arthur so he had NO legal claim to anything. It was all based on my personal relationship with him and the level of trust I had in our friendship. Nia tried to warn me numerous times, but I wouldn't listen.

"Melvin, he is NOT our friend!" she would say, pleading with me not to trust him. My response would always be the same.

"Nah, you just don't know. That is my dude. There are a lot of things I might have to worry about but I know for a fact I ain't got to worry about Arthur stealing from me. Ain't no way he would do something like that." I was, quite possibly, the dumbest son-of-a-bitch in the history of the promotions business.

Keep in mind, when this all started Arthur was broke, sleeping on Nia's couch. The only money he made during that time came from the show, of which he legally owned ZERO percent. The only deal we EVER signed was for Baci to own 50% and for us to own 50%. Arthur NEVER owned anything. So it was all mine and Nia's money after Baci left minus whatever piece was sold to a promoter to pay the expenses for a certain city or date. So if Arthur was the promoter in a city, he should have paid those expenses out of his pocket AND split whatever came back with me and Nia. Only he had no money to pay for any expenses. He used ours and since he controlled the finances, he kept most of what came back for himself, only giving us enough to keep us quiet.

It took me a while to figure it out, and to be honest I didn't piece it all together until months later. By the time we got to Houston however, I did know we were getting ripped off and had every intention of going over that paperwork with a fine tooth comb to ensure we got paid something close to what we were owed. Arthur couldn't have that. He already had plans for that money . . .

To put things in perspective, we did two successful shows at the Fox in Atlanta and walked away with a couple hundred thousand dollars. Tyler and Arthur did SIXTEEN successful shows in Houston. And with me and Nia out of the deal, Arthur got to keep every dime of that money because, you guessed it, he was the promoter in that city.

From the beginning, our biggest problem was a lack of resources. Well, from that point on, money was no longer an issue for Tyler or Arthur, and it never would be again. Shortly after wrapping up a successful run in Houston, Tyler got to work his next production, "I Can Do Bad All By Myself" produced by Arthur Primas.

CHAPTER
22

I Know I've Been Changed

I tried calling Tyler but since I couldn't get him on the phone, I had no choice but to hire a lawyer to look at the situation in Houston. He charged me a $7,500 retainer to tell me that the case could cost as much as $25,000 to litigate, depending on their response. I only had about $10,000 left at that point so I was at a crossroads. I could scrape and scrounge up enough money to go forward with the legal action, or I could just walk away. Neither of those choices appealed to me AT ALL.

How in the hell was I supposed to just walk away from something that I had worked and fought this hard for? I gave up several years of my life chasing this thing only to have it stolen from me the minute it was beginning to pay off, and now I was supposed to just eat shit and let the person who stole it reap the rewards of my sacrifices? Hell no! I literally took food out of my family's mouth to hold this thing together until we made it to the House of Blues, and I was supposed to just step aside and allow my contribution to be forgotten? I wasn't having any of that. Arthur was gonna give me every damn dime he owed me.

I wasn't walking away from a damn thing, at least that was my ego talking. My head was saying something completely different.

When I removed myself from the emotion of the moment and just looked at things logically, it really wasn't a difficult decision. I knew that I could, and probably would, win a civil suit. Arthur had no leg to stand on, as we had never signed anything with him. But I also had no visibility to the box office numbers so I had no idea how much money was going to be there for me to make a claim to. Besides, I knew that Arthur had cooked those books so thoroughly that it would have taken ten forensic accountants several months to figure out what was the real number and what wasn't. Even then, who knew how much was rightfully mine? I couldn't afford to spend the last little bit of money I had only to recoup a few thousand dollars, a year or more down the road. The more I thought about it, the more it became clear. I really only had one choice, I had to walk away.

There was one more reason I ultimately decided to walk away, it was already over. Yes, whatever money was made in Houston rightfully belonged to Nia and myself but beyond that, there really was nothing else to hold on to. Tyler had made the decision to move on and, to be fair, when you look at what he has done since those days, who in their right mind could make an argument that he made the wrong decision? Whatever part God had in mind for me to play in Tyler's career had obviously run its course, and it was time for both of us to move on.

That hasn't always been an easy road for me. Walking away from that show did not kill my ambition. If anything,

I was fueled even more to get back in the game and rise to the top. I immediately wanted to start chasing the dream again, only this time I would be smarter and more focused. I would take what I learned from this experience and nobody would be able to stop me. I was born to do this; it was my destiny. It would take me a few more years to realize what I was chasing didn't exist.

> *. . . peace I leave with you; my peace I give you.*
> *I do not give you as the world gives.*
> —John 14:27

One of the things you realize, as you get older is that so much of what we say and do in youth is all about how others see us. What I was chasing had nothing to do with my destiny and everything to do with my own insecurities. I wanted the people around me to see me as successful, and I was willing to do whatever it took to create that persona. In hindsight I know that the damage I've done to those closest to me could never have been rectified simply by making a bunch of money. I know now that it is the content of my character that I want to shape other people's view of me and, in that, I have found peace with what happened all those years ago.

You can ask Tyler or Arthur tomorrow and neither one of them will say that I stole from them, that I cheated them or took advantage of them in any way. I made more than my share of mistakes, but I was doing the best I could for all of us. Knowing that, I can live comfortably with my place in the history of Tyler Perry, even if he cannot.

Yes I was doing it for my own selfish reasons and yes, had it not been me Tyler would have possibly been discovered by someone else. But it was me and not anyone else who discovered Tyler Perry. It was me who took the chance and made the sacrifices to make it happen for him, and for that, I am grateful.

The other thing you realize, as you get older is that, in life, you always regret those things you don't do far more than the things you do. You learn to treasure all of life's experiences, good and bad, because they are the things that shape you into the person you will ultimately become. I'm just a knucklehead from Oklahoma City, and I got to play a pivotal role in the launching of the career of the one of the most powerful entertainers in the history of Black America. Was it easy? Hell no. Did it benefit me financially? Not even close but I literally had a front row seat to the making of history. More than a front row seat, I got to be the driving force in the very beginning when it was far from a sure thing. Tyler Perry trusted me with his career long before you could legitimately even call it a career and look where he is now. For that experience, how can I be anything but thankful?

Whatever I have made of my life since then has been greatly influenced by what happened all those years ago. Don't get me wrong, I remain, very much, a work in progress, but I am at peace with the man I am and the man I am becoming. As hurt and as disillusioned as I was when it all went down, I can look back now and say with confidence that I wouldn't have done a single thing differently. I considered someone to be a friend and so I trusted him. I honestly wouldn't want to be the kind of person who wouldn't have done that. I made plenty of mistakes, but that wasn't one of them.

In the end, my initial feelings about Tyler and his talent have been validated many times over. I knew he was a special talent and it was my privilege to work with him and help him get started. And while he may not value my contribution to where he is today, I am more than comfortable letting you decide for yourself how significant my role was.

As for my family and all those who have stuck with me through all of this, I want to say thank you and I love you. Things may not have worked out the way I wanted, but God's plan has always been better than my own. And that's what this book is really about.

Because while I cannot say that Tyler Perry wouldn't have become who he is without Melvin Childs, I can absolutely say that Melvin Childs NEVER WOULD HAVE MADE IT without you.